*Short Bike Rides™ Series*

# Short Bike Rides™ in Wisconsin

*By*

Greg Marr

An East Woods Book

The Globe Pequot Press

Old Saybrook, Connecticut

**Library of Congress Cataloging-in-Publication Data**

Marr, Greg.
  Short bike rides in Wisconsin / Greg Marr.
      p.    cm. — (Short bike rides series)
  ISBN 0-7627-0046-7
  1. Bicycle touring—Wisconsin—Guidebooks. 2. Wisconsin—Guidebooks.
I. Title. II. Series
  GV1045.5.W6M27   1997
  796.6'4'09775—dc21                                                97-13800
                                                                          CIP

✪ This book is printed on recycled paper.
Manufactured in the United States of America
First Edition/First Printing

For George and Janet Marr, who put me on my

first bicycle and guided me down the path

that led to this book

# About the Author

A lifelong Wisconsin resident, Greg Marr has bicycled Wisconsin's back roads for twenty-five years. He is the founder and editor of the Wisconsin-based *Silent Sports*, a monthly Midwest regional magazine devoted to bicycling and other forms of self-propelled recreation. He is also a regional editor for *EcoTraveler*, a magazine on ecologically friendly worldwide travel.

# Feedback

Let me know what you think of these rides or if you have suggestions for other rides to be included in future editions of this book. Also, errors are possible. If you've found any, or have discovered that some roads have been renamed, be sure to let me know. Write to me c/o The Globe Pequot Press, P.O. Box 833, Old Saybrook, CT 06475.

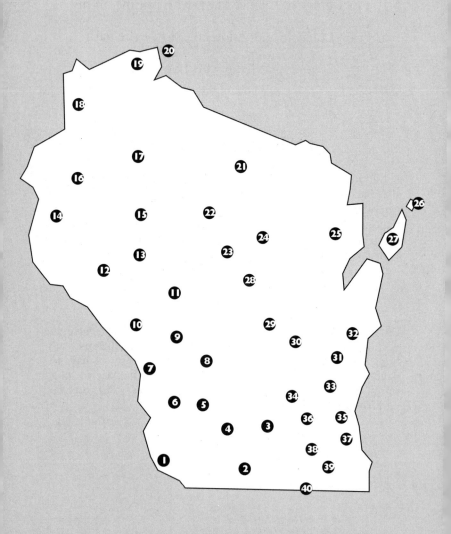

# Contents

Introduction ................................................................................................. vi

The Rides
1. Mississippi Meander ................................................................. 1
2. The Swiss Scene/Sugar River Trail .......................................... 5
3. Mad City Capitol Cruise ......................................................... 11
4. Mount Horeb Mound Bounding ............................................. 17
5. A Wright-Stuff Ride ................................................................ 23
6. Ocooch Mountain Climb ........................................................ 29
7. Amish Country Amble ............................................................ 35
8. Weaving through Wisconsin's Alps ........................................ 41
9. Tunnel Vision: Elroy-Sparta Trail — and More .................... 47
10. Touring Trempealeau and the Garden of Eden ...................... 51
11. Homage to the Highground ................................................... 58
12. Red Cedar Ramble ................................................................. 65
13. Chippin' Away at Lake Wissota ............................................. 71
14. St. Croix Freefall ................................................................... 77
15. Blue Hills Ascent ................................................................... 85
16. Webster Tour of Lakes ........................................................... 91
17. Hayward Lakes: Where Eagles Soar ...................................... 95
18. Waterfall Wander .................................................................. 101
19. Bayfield Orchard Blast .......................................................... 105
20. Riding with the Apostles ....................................................... 111
21. Minocqua Lakes and Bearskin Trail Loop ............................ 117
22. Timm's Hill Turnaround ....................................................... 125
23. Ginseng Country Tour ........................................................... 129
24. Lakewood and the Nicolet National Forest ........................... 135
25. The Crivitz Cruise ................................................................. 141
26. Death's Door to Washington Island ...................................... 147
27. Crossing Door Shore to Shore ............................................... 153
28. A Dip by the Eau Claire Dells ............................................... 159
29. River City Ramble ................................................................. 163
30. Hartman Creek/Chain O' Lakes Cruise ................................. 169
31. Escaping the Escarpment ...................................................... 175
32. A Tale of Two Rivers ............................................................. 181
33. North Kettles Cruise .............................................................. 185
34. Yachts of Fun at Green Lake .................................................. 191
35. The Sites of Cedarburg .......................................................... 195
36. Pike Lake and Those Holy Hills ............................................ 201
37. Milwaukee: Mansions, Lake Michigan, and the 76 Trail ....... 207
38. Tour de Fort .......................................................................... 213
39. Chocolate City Delight .......................................................... 219
40. Roun'da Manure and More .................................................... 225

Organizations, Resources, and Clubs ......................... 230-33
Annual Wisconsin Bike Rides .................................. 233-42

# Introduction

For all the spectacular bicycling in Wisconsin, we can thank two things: the forces of nature and the needs of humankind.

Eons ago what we now know as Wisconsin was vastly different. Geologists believe that there was once a range of mountains in northern Wisconsin that would rival the present-day Rockies. Forces of nature—earthquakes, volcanoes, floods, wind, and storms—pounded away at these majestic mountains for millions of years, but nothing did more to shape the terrain than glaciers. Massive sheets of ice inched across Wisconsin, slowly retreated, and then came back again. The mountains, like everything else, fell to the glaciers. The last glacier to do its damage retreated 10,000 years ago, a mere speck of time in geological terms, but it was kind enough to leave behind an incredible natural playground for outdoor enthusiasts.

The last glacier, called the Wisconsin Glacier, did not completely cover the state. The southwestern quarter of Wisconsin, known as the Driftless Area, was untouched. The hills and deep valleys of the Driftless Area escaped that last crushing blow, resulting in an Appalachian type of rolling countryside.

The other major factor that makes Wisconsin an ideal bicycling destination is found in the slogan that graces every automobile license plate in the state, "America's Dairyland." Much of rural Wisconsin, particularly in the more temperate bottom two-thirds of the state, is farm country, and most of the farms are dairy farms. What distinguishes dairy farms from other farms is that the "produce" has to be taken to market every day. No matter the weather (and it can be severe in Wisconsin), milk is hauled every day of the year; and consequently, a reliable system of roads—one that can be counted on in rain, snow, and sleet—is a necessity. What this means for the bicyclist is an excellent system of paved back roads.

Wisconsin's back roads were engineered to bring milk to market, not for speed or terrain. Ribbons of asphalt wrap up, over, and around hills and connect farms to small towns and small towns to large cities. Although bicycle riding was not considered when these roadways were laid out for their initial utilitarian purpose, the roadways couldn't be much better if they were specifically designed with bicycling in mind.

Bicyclists anywhere in the state will encounter, to varying degrees, the influence of the glaciers. As a glacier moves along its slow path, it freezes anything in its way, picks up bedrock, and scours the land with boulders. When it begins its slow retreat, it leaves this glacial garbage behind in a long, rambling ridge known as a moraine. The leading edge of the glacier, called a terminal moraine, can be easily seen in Wisconsin as a reasonably distinct series of ridges that run up the center of the state and then swing west across the north-central area. The glacier did not retreat uniformly, however; it paused occasionally, leaving smaller piles of debris. Nor were glaciers one solid chuck of ice; rather, there were several "lobes" of ice rubbing against one another, leaving behind still other features. The result is that much of Wisconsin can be referred to in glacial terminology: moraines, kettles, drumlins, and eskers—all terms that define the variety of landscapes found in the state.

What you will find as you tour Wisconsin is a remarkable diversity. In addition to the glacial landscape features, Wisconsin's northern location gives it several very distinct ecological zones, each with unique features. As you travel across the state, you will encounter boreal forests, swamps, ranges of mini-mountains, two of the Great Lakes, the Mississippi River, and thousands of inland lakes, rivers, and streams. Some people say you can't bicycle year-round in Wisconsin, but a few hardy souls insist on turning pedals throughout our winter months. We don't really mind winter—it gives us a chance to overhaul our bikes while we cross-country ski.

Finally, there are the people of Wisconsin. Small, friendly towns seem to appear just around the bend when a weary cyclist needs a place to stop for a drink or a meal. Larger cities, like Madison and Milwaukee, are graced with bike paths and parkways. Tourism is the second leading industry in the state, so, almost everywhere you go, there are people and services to make you feel welcome. "America's Dairyland"? "America's Bicycling Paradise" is more like it.

# About the Rides

Suggesting where to ride is a subjective undertaking; most bicycling guide books are the creation of one or two bicycling enthusiasts who offer their favorite choices in a given area. With more than twenty years of bicycling experience in Wisconsin, I certainly have my favorite places to ride, but, to set this book apart from others, I went to the people involved in bicycling across Wisconsin: the clubs, organizations, and bike-ride organizers. Who better to know the best places to ride than the people who actually live there?

To that end, the rides presented here are the result of a collaborative effort. I asked people around the state to provide me with their favorite rides, and they responded. My job was to select the best of the lot. Some criteria for the selection were determined by the publisher: for instance, rides ranging in length from 10 to 30 miles. My criteria were scenery and geography. Wisconsin is a diverse state, ranging from large metropolitan areas to quaint small towns, the Great Lakes to small inland lakes, cultivated farmland to near wilderness, hills rivaling mountains to flatland resembling prairies. My goal was to celebrate the geographic diversity of the state while providing the best of scenery in each area.

The end product is a collection of forty rides, two-thirds of which were recommended by the bike riders of Wisconsin. Even with the routes I selected, I found many were local favorites used by clubs and often, in part at least, as routes for annual rides. I personally checked out every route given here, including those suggested by others. I occasionally tweaked the suggested route, adding a road here, eliminating a road there, or combining parts of several suggested routes.

There are, no doubt, rides missing from this list that surely qualify as a "best" 10-to-30-mile route. Picking the best short bike rides in Wisconsin is essentially a process of elimination, and a difficult one at that. My long list, the one used to narrow down to these forty, had more than seventy potential rides. In the end I even eliminated two of my personal favorites at the last minute in favor of equally good rides in other parts of the state.

Whatever your preconceived notions may be about Wisconsin, do not think that it is flat because it is a Midwestern state distinctly out of any major mountain range (its highest point is a mere 2,000 feet above sea level). The truth is that very little of Wisconsin can be termed flat. Wisconsin is almost all hills, and riders of bicycles inevitably encounter them in all but a few areas of the state.

Wisconsin's hills can be deceptively challenging. Although they are not as long as those you'd find in mountain states, they often come at you one after another after another in roller-coaster fashion. How hilly can Wisconsin be? Consider that there is a group of riders in the state who, each year, pour over contour maps of southwestern Wisconsin in search of a single 100-mile ride that will contain 10,000 feet of elevation gain. Although they haven't found it yet, they've come close—more than 10,000 feet in 115 miles.

Fortunately, not all of Wisconsin is quite that hilly, although several rides in this book are in that hilly section of the state called Coulee Country, whose hills and hidden valleys, although slow-going on a bike, offer some of the most outstanding scenery in all of the Midwest.

Many of these rides use Wisconsin's outstanding system of state parks as starting points. Besides offering wonderful facilities, each park has convenient places to leave your car. There is, however, a daily fee charged for park use, or you can buy an annual car-windshield sticker that allows entrance to all parks. Daily or annual stickers can be purchased at each park or by mail from Wisconsin Park and Recreation, P.O. Box 7921, Madison, WI 53707–7921; (608) 266–2621. Of course, these rides can be joined anywhere along their length.

Wisconsin is the nation's leader in rail-trail miles, and a number of the rides here include portions of rail-trails. A book could be written on rail-trails alone in Wisconsin, with more than 700 miles of them in the state; but, unfortunately, all rail-trails are point-to-point rides. *The rides listed here are all loops,* bringing the rider back to the starting point. Therefore, only short sections of rail-trails were used here as part of a longer loop. Passes are required for rail-trails and are available at trail heads or from Wisconsin Park and Recreation, P.O. Box 7921, Madison, WI 53707–7921. The cost is $10.00 per calendar year, $3.00 daily.

Keep in mind that more adventurous cyclists may want to use these rides as a portion of a longer ride. For instance, the Bayfield tour is a short but demanding 10-mile ride; a longer ride of nearly 50 miles can be taken around the tip of the peninsula and back to the original short ride. Get a detailed county map and be creative.

# Enjoying the Rides

Before setting out on any of these rides, keep in mind two things: Bicycle computers and odometers often vary, and road signs change. On the Bearskin Trail, for instance, I found my computer off by two-tenths of a mile from the officially posted trail signs. The difference may seem insignificant in a 10-mile ride; but, in a 30-miler, a couple of tenths toward the end of a long ride might mean a wrong turn.

Many Wisconsin counties are in the process of changing road names: A road name printed here today might not be there tomorrow. When in doubt, stop and ask someone. Wisconsin is a bicycle-friendly state, and residents are generally quite helpful.

To help keep you on the right road, each of the rides includes both a detailed cue sheet, "Directions for the Ride," and a general map. The maps are not drawn to scale, *nor do they include every small street or railroad crossing encountered*—in some cases, they're noted on the cue sheets for convenience. Using the maps and cue sheets together, however, should overcome bicycle-computer differences and renamed roads to eliminate any likelihood of taking a wrong turn.

## Maintenance and Repairs

A properly maintained bike should carry you through a season with little problem, except for flats. Even if you can't tell a down tube from a pedal, at least be able to fix a flat. If you don't know how, ask at your local bike shop; I don't know of any shop that won't help a customer learn this most basic of repair skills. Practice at home before you have to do a roadside repair. The basics: Carry a pump, a spare tube, and the tools necessary to remove the wheel and tire. I also carry a patch kit in case I have more than one flat.

Beyond flats, it's a good idea to get to know your bike well enough to perform simple adjustments and bolt tightening. Things do rattle loose, and it's better to be able to fix them on the road than it is to pray they hold up until you get back to your car. Check with local retailers and/or clubs for information on basic repair classes.

In a worst-case scenario, keep in mind that you are not in the wilderness. If something happens to your bike and you can't continue, flag a passing car or walk to the nearest house.

## Dogs

In "America's Dairyland," it seems that every other farm has a critter or two running loose. Most dogs bark merely to tell you that you are passing through their territory. A few, however, are downright nasty, vile creatures. How you deal with them is a matter of personal preference. I find that a loud, firm "Stay!" or "No!" at least slows them down long enough for me to cruise on by. Sometimes a squirt of a water bottle between the eyes does the trick, but your aim has to be good. Some people prefer a blast from a commercially available repellent.

If you see that you simply are not going to be able to outride a dog, and it appears to be of the vile, nasty variety, get off your bike—keeping it between you and the animal—and walk out of its territory. *Be sure to report the incident to the authorities,* and press your case. Wisconsin has a law about animals running loose.

## Bags

A ride of 10 to 30 miles need not require much in the way of additional gear. A single bag—handlebar, rack or top tube—should be all you need to carry food, a light jacket, and personal items like sunglasses, sunscreen, car keys, and money. Handlebar bags with plastic map holders are convenient to help you follow along the route.

## Food and Water

Most of the rides can be handled with nothing more than a single water bottle, as food stops are frequent on all but a few rides. On longer rides it's a good idea to take a snack. High-energy bars and fruit are good choices.

## Helmets

There is no Wisconsin law that requires the use of a helmet; common sense shouldn't have to be legislated. Think head, think pavement, think of being in a vegetative state for the rest of your life, or worse, if your bare head connects with the pavement at 20 miles per hour. Use your head now to save it for later. In other words, use a good helmet. The best are ones that meet ANZI or SNELL safety standards.

## Clothing

Bike shorts were not designed to look goofy; they look goofy for a very practical reason. There's a soft pad between you and your bike saddle, and the tight fit keeps clothing from rubbing against your skin. If the Lycra look isn't for you, looser-fitting padded shorts are also available. Bike jerseys that are made from fabrics that wick away moisture and have rear cargo pockets are also functional. Padded gloves are a must for two reasons: The pads cushion your palms on the handlebars, and the gloves protect your hands in case of a fall.

Whatever clothing you choose, make it as bright and visible as possible. You don't want to blend into your surroundings with two-ton vehicles whizzing by—you want to be seen. Bright clothing is critical should you happen to be on the road near or past sundown. If you anticipate riding in the dark, at the very least have front and rear reflectors. Battery-powered front and rear lights are even better (the rear red light should blink).

## Ride Defensively

Ride as if you were invisible—which, to many motor-vehicle operators, you are. Many motorists just do not see cyclists. They're looking for cars and trucks moving at the speed limit, not bikes poking along at 10 miles per hour. Sure, you have as much right to the road as they do, but that doesn't mean a heck of a lot when you collide with a car. Take the responsibility to ride defensively and look out for them.

## Parked Cars

One of my greatest fears of urban riding is getting "doored"—passing a parked car at the moment the door swings open. I try to scan parked cars to see if there are occupants on the driver's side. Wherever traffic permits, I try to stay a door's length away from parked cars. It's perfectly legal to travel in the traffic lane, and it's advisable to do so when passing parked cars.

## The Road

At the time this book was being researched, all the routes given here were paved, but this doesn't mean they've stayed in good condition. Be on the lookout for construction work and potholes. Watch out for sandy gravel on corners—it's easy to overlook a slick patch of gravel on a corner and end up meeting the pavement. I know; I've done it.

## Laws

Obey all traffic laws. Not only does compliance with the law make cyclists look good as fellow road users, it's safer for you and the motorists. Stop at signs and lights. Use hand signals in traffic. Don't ride up onto sidewalks to avoid stoplights. Use common sense.

## Locks

Whether to carry a lock or not is a matter of personal preference. If you feel uncomfortable leaving your bike untended for even a few minutes while you visit a rest room, use a lock. Peace of mind, in the manner of a heavy U-bolt lock, is better than constant worry. Bike thieves abound, and theft can happen in the most unlikely of places.

# Acknowledgments

This book is truly a collaborative effort. Bicyclists from throughout the state as well as organizers of bike rides offered advice, shared maps and cue sheets, and encouraged me in this project; the support of the entire Wisconsin bicycling community was overwhelming. The final selection of rides in this book was mine, but, without all of these people's input, the book would not have been nearly as complete.

For help on specific rides, I thank Randy Alt, Jane Bidwell, Bob Bellamy, Chris Black, Rosalie Ceschi, Sarah Detling, Dan Clausen, Randy Fabian, Michelle Feiber, Richard Haughian, Debby Henning, Bill Johnson, Tina Karas, Bob Koldeway, Paul Lata, Paul Matty, Olga McAnulty, Liz McBride, John McKenzie, Mike Meuret, Dennis Northey, Collen E. O'Neil, Tom Opect, David Peterson, Allan Rindahl, Michael D. Stumpf, Jean Toney, David Waraxa, and the Bombay Bicycle Club.

Additional thanks to Laura Strom, my editor, for the opportunity and the encouragement throughout this project; and Phil Van Valkenberg, *the* authority on bicycling in Wisconsin, for his help and advice; Carl Knuese, of Campus Cycle, who was there at the beginning and never faltered in his encouragement; Greg Ott, who taught me more about bike maintenance than he'll ever know; Gomez, with whom I took my first "long" bike ride; Scott Turner, for the freedom to work on this book; and Jon Hansen, for help with the photographs.

Special thanks to my frequent touring companions—Joel Fisher, Greg Stadler, and Paul West. The miles we've bicycled together on the roads of Wisconsin were the basis for this book.

Finally, my love and heartfelt thanks to my wife, Martha Fullmer, and stepchildren, Amanda and David Fullmer, for enduring my absences and giving me the time to complete this project.

# Mississippi Meander

| | |
|---:|:---|
| **Number of miles:** | 13.3 (16.5 with visit to Nelson Dewey State Park) |
| **Approximate pedaling time:** | 1.5 hours |
| **Terrain:** | Challenging; several big hills |
| **Traffic:** | Light |
| **Things to see:** | Mississippi River, Stonefield Village, Nelson Dewey State Park |
| **Food:** | In Cassville |

Cassville, a quaint Mississippi River town that calls to mind the days of Mark Twain, is accentuated by huge wooded bluffs that rise up from both sides of the river for an isolated, time-forgotten feeling. On the surface Cassville would seem to be no more important than any other small river town, but it played an important role in Wisconsin's history. Nelson Dewey, a young lawyer from Cassville, was Wisconsin's first governor. He is remembered through a state park named after him. Nelson Dewey State Park is located 1.6 miles north of Cassville along the Mississippi River. Just across from the park is Stonefield Village, a facsimile of a late 19th-century village that includes restorations of Dewey's home and farm buildings.

Although this ride is short, it is challenging. The hill country of southeastern Wisconsin requires strong legs, a strong heart, and multiple gearing to negotiate the many ups and downs. Some argue that a weak mind helps as well.

Start at Riverside Park on the banks of the Mississippi. Keep an eye peeled for waterfowl and majestic bald eagles flying overhead. To the north of the park is a ferry that can shuttle you across to the Iowa side.

Before you leave, make sure your brakes are in good working

I

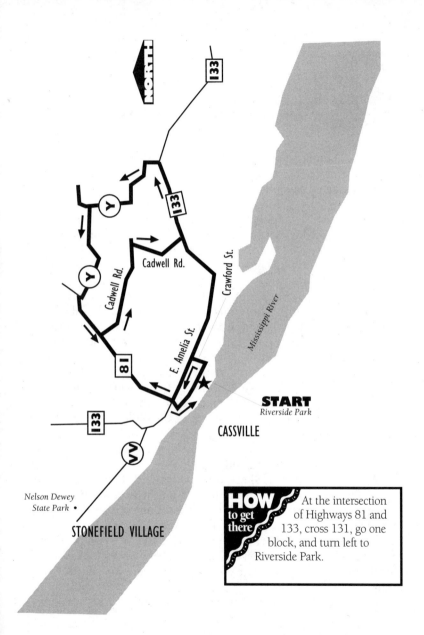

NORTH

133

Y

Y

Cadwell Rd.

Cadwell Rd.

Crawford St.

Mississippi River

81

E. Amelia St.

133

VV

START
*Riverside Park*

CASSVILLE

*Nelson Dewey
State Park* •

STONEFIELD VILLAGE

**HOW** to get there — At the intersection of Highways 81 and 133, cross 131, go one block, and turn left to Riverside Park.

**DIREC-TIONS at a glance**

0.0  Exit Riverside Park parking lot and turn onto Crawford Street.
0.2  Turn left onto East Amelia Street.
0.5  Turn right onto Highway 81.
2.5  Turn right onto Cadwell Road.
5.1  Turn left onto Highway 133.
6.5  Turn left onto County Y.
10.1  Turn left onto Highway 81.
12.7  Cross Highway 133.
12.8  Turn left onto Front Street.
13.3  Turn right into parking lot.

**For the 16.5-mile option**
Follow directions for shorter ride through 12.7 miles.
12.7  After returning to Cassville, turn right onto Highway 133.
13.3  Turn left onto County VV.
14.3  Enter state park. Retrace route to Riverside Park.
16.5  Turn right into parking lot.

order; you'll need them to control your speed on some of the hills on this ride.

Exit the park on the south end on Crawford Street. Go west (away from the river) two blocks, turn left on East Amelia Street (Highway 133), then right onto Highway 81. Take a deep breath, shift down, and begin the ascent. Although this is a state highway, traffic is not heavy, and the road is fairly wide. After climbing for a while, the highway dips slightly before topping out at 2 miles. A small downhill leads to a right turn on Cadwell Road.

Catch your breath here and enjoy a steep downhill to 2.9 miles through wooded countryside. A curving climb up is rewarded with a wonderful view, the first of many, at 3.5 miles. To the right you can see the bluffs on the far side of the Mississippi.

Cadwell bends to the right at 4.1 miles for yet another stunning view.

At 5.1 miles turn left onto Highway 133, where there's a good downhill to a creek crossing at 5.4 miles, then another climb. At 6.5 miles turn left onto County Y.

County Y rolls up and down, following the rugged terrain, as it passes through farm fields. The views are exceptional all the way to Highway 81 at 10.1 miles. At 7.7 miles there's a sharp turn to right, then a good drop down. At 8.1 miles the road turns right at a hilltop, drops for nearly a half mile, then leads into another uphill.

Coming back into town on Highway 81 gives you the opportunity to enjoy the grinding hill you climbed up to start the ride. Pass Cadwell Road on the left at 10.8 miles, climb the little hill in front of you, and then get ready for a coast back to town. Cross Highway 133, go one block, and then turn left on Front Street at 12.8 miles. The parking lot is a half mile ahead on the right.

To take a side trip to Nelson Dewey State Park and Stonefield Village, turn right from Highway 81 onto Highway 133 for six-tenths of a mile to the stop at County VV. Go left on VV 1 mile to the park. Return the same way.

Tour the village and Dewey's estate or walk through the trails at the park, where wildlife, waterfowl, and songbirds are in abundance. A road weaves around some Hopewell Indian burial mounds, and a trail leads to a bluff with an excellent overlook of the Mississippi River.

# The Swiss Scene/ Sugar River Trail

| | |
|---:|:---|
| **Number of miles:** | 16.9 |
| **Approximate pedaling time:** | 2 hours |
| **Terrain:** | Flat on trail; rolling elsewhere, with two challenging climbs |
| **Traffic:** | Light |
| **Things to see:** | Sugar River Trail, New Glarus, Swiss Historic Village Museum, numerous Swiss-related attractions, restaurant, shops |
| **Food:** | New Glarus; Monticello at 6.8 miles |

One look at the small town of New Glarus and you'll see why it is aptly named "America's Little Switzerland." Swiss-style architecture abounds along the highway coming toward New Glarus and up and down the two-block-long Main Street. The Swiss Historic Village Museum looks down from a hillside on the west edge of New Glarus, and at least a dozen original and replica buildings provide an authentic Swiss feel to your visit. The Chalet of the Golden Fleece Museum displays wood carvings, jewelry, and other baubles. The Swiss Miss Lace Factory turns out Swiss lace and embroideries on looms imported from the homeland. Feast on Swiss food at several restaurants and stay in Swiss chalets while you bike in the area. If you hit it just right, there might be a festival over the weekend, perhaps even a performance of the *Wilhelm Tell Drama.*

Swiss settlers, 108 of them, first came to the area in the 1840s. They found a place to their liking, one with rich farmland, and wrote home to relatives. Soon this rolling hill country

Welcome

Wisconsin
State Trails

of south-central Wisconsin had more than 1,000 transplanted Swiss bringing their culture to the Midwest. All that was missing was mountains, thankfully for us, although the area is hilly enough to make for an interesting ride.

We begin in New Glarus on the Sugar River Trail, a limestone-surfaced rail-trail that runs from New Glarus 23.5 miles southeast to Brodhead. There's a spur that leads to New Glarus Woods State Park, a couple of miles due south. If you don't have an annual pass for State Trails, pay $3.00 at the converted railroad depot and head out.

Stay to the left where the sign points to New Glarus Woods State Park, cross the highway, and you'll cross a wooden bridge before a road crossing at 1 mile. You'll follow roughly along the Little Sugar River, crossing it (or streams feeding it) several times. The second mile is through open fields and wetlands, with a power line overhead to the left. At 2.5 miles pass through a more wooded area, with trees next to the trail. Stop and cross Exeter Crossing Road at 3.8 miles—the small town of Exeter is just to the left—before the forest closes in between 4 and 5 miles. At County C, 6 miles, turn right and leave the trail behind.

You're not anywhere near the Swiss Alps, but there will be some climbing now that you're off the trail. The first climb is up into Monticello. At 6.8 miles stop, then turn left onto Main Street, cross Highway 39 at 7 miles, then turn right onto County C at 7.1 miles. There's a river pond off to the right. Cross Highway 69/39 at 7.4 miles and continue out County C to the west.

Begin this section with a gradual uphill. There's no paved shoulder, but the road is good, with little traffic. At 7.7 miles the road flattens out before getting into some not-too-severe ups and downs; the countryside is all rolling hills and farm fields. Begin a climb up at 9.8 miles; then enjoy a wonderful downhill run starting at 10.2 miles.

Turn right onto County N at 10.5 miles for a downhill, then a gradual winding climb up that goes on for almost a mile and a half. The payoff for this is some stunning views of the surrounding countryside from a ridgetop and a fun roller-coaster ride.

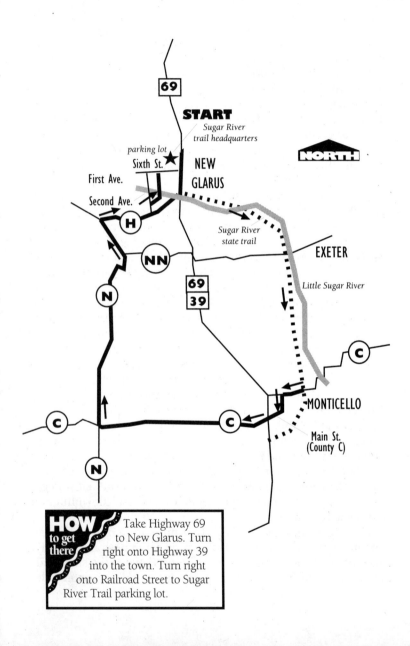

**69**

**START**

*Sugar River trail headquarters*

*parking lot*

Sixth St. ★

**NEW GLARUS**

First Ave.

Second Ave.

**NORTH**

**H**

*Sugar River state trail*

**NN**

**EXETER**

**N**

**69 39**

*Little Sugar River*

**C**

**C**

**C**

**MONTICELLO**

**C**

Main St. (County C)

**N**

**HOW** to get there   Take Highway 69 to New Glarus. Turn right onto Highway 39 into the town. Turn right onto Railroad Street to Sugar River Trail parking lot.

**DIREC-TIONS at a glance**

| | |
|---|---|
| 0.0 | Enter Sugar River Trail from headquarters parking lot. Follow trail for 6 miles. |
| 6.0 | Exit trail with right turn onto County C. |
| 6.8 | Turn left onto Main Street. |
| 7.0 | Cross Highway 39. |
| 7.1 | Turn right onto County C. |
| 7.4 | Cross Highway 69/39. |
| 10.5 | Turn right onto County N. |
| 13.6 | Continue on County N (bear left) at intersection with County NN. |
| 14.4 | Turn right onto County H. |
| 15.7 | Turn left onto Second Avenue (no sign; turn just before getting to Highway 69/39). |
| 15.1 | Turn right onto First Avenue. |
| 16.0 | Turn right onto Sixth Street. |
| 16.6 | Turn left onto Railroad Street (not shown on map). |
| 16.9 | Continue to parking lot for Sugar River Trail. |

You go right, left, up, and down while enjoying the scenery.

At 13.6 miles turn left onto N at the intersection with County NN; the latter will take you to New Glarus Woods State Park. Continue on N to a stop at 14.4 miles and make a right turn on County H. Almost immediately you'll enjoy a mile-long fun, swooping ride to the right, then back to the left, before it begins to flatten out at 15.2 miles.

Just before you come up on Highway 69/39, turn left on the unmarked road at 15.7 miles. This is Second Avenue, which leads back into New Glarus. At about 15.7 miles veer right onto First Avenue to a stop at Sixth Street at 16 miles and make a right turn. Go through town to a left turn onto Railroad Street at 16.6 miles and then back to your car in the trail-head parking lot at 16.9 miles.

# Mad City Capitol Cruise

| | |
|---:|:---|
| **Number of miles:** | 15.8 |
| **Approximate pedaling time:** | 2 hours |
| **Terrain:** | Generally flat, with a couple of tough hills |
| **Traffic:** | None on paths; moderate on city streets |
| **Things to see:** | Lake Mendota, Lake Monona, Lake Wingra, University of Wisconsin, State Street pedestrian mall, University of Wisconsin Arboretum, Wisconsin State Capitol |
| **Food:** | Throughout the ride; best on State Street |

In 1996 Madison, Wisconsin's capital and home to the University of Wisconsin, was named the most "livable" city in the country by *Fortune* magazine. Madison has not only all the cultural benefits of a big city—theaters and the performing arts, ethnic restaurants, and art exhibits—but also the charms of a much smaller town. Surrounded by lakes, Madison boasts 200 parks, more than a dozen beaches, botanical gardens, and a zoo. This ride highlights some of Madison's best features.

One reason for Madison's lofty status as the most livable city in the United States is its commitment to bicycling. Madison is extremely bike-friendly, with designated bike lanes on major roads and numerous bike paths throughout the city. The ride begins on the west side of the city at Rennebohn Park at Regent and Eau Claire Streets. Park along Eau Claire Street or in the lot

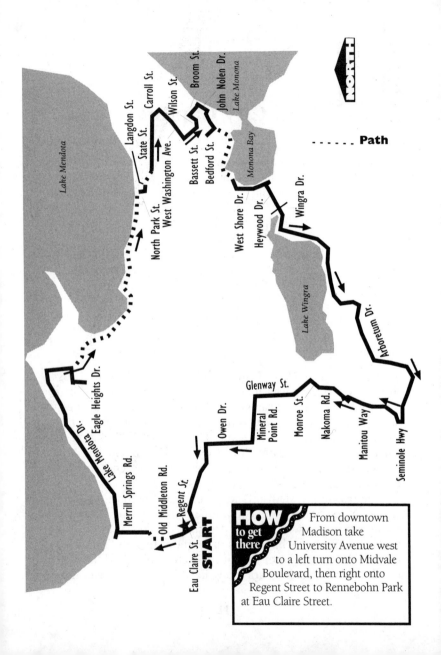

NORTH

····· **Path**

*Lake Mendota*

*Lake Monona*

*Monona Bay*

*Lake Wingra*

Langdon St.
Carroll St.
State St.
Wilson St.
Broom St.
John Nolen Dr.
Bassett St.
Bedford St.
North Park St.
West Washington Ave.
West Shore Dr.
Heywood Dr.
Wingra Dr.
Arboretum Dr.
Eagle Heights Dr.
Glenway St.
Owen Dr.
Mineral Point Rd.
Monroe St.
Nakoma Rd.
Manitou Way
Seminole Hwy
Lake Mendota Dr.
Merrill Springs Rd.
Old Middleton Rd.
Regent St.
Eau Claire St.
**START**

**HOW** to get there  From downtown Madison take University Avenue west to a left turn onto Midvale Boulevard, then right onto Regent Street to Rennebohn Park at Eau Claire Street.

**DIREC-TIONS at a glance**

0.0 At intersection of Eau Claire and Regent Streets at Rennebohn Park, go north on Eau Claire Street.

0.2 Cross Sheboygan Avenue.

0.4 Cross Old Middleton Road to bike path.

0.5 Take path to the right around park.

0.6 Go straight on Merrill Springs Road.

1.0 Turn right on Lake Mendota Drive.

1.7 Stay left on Lake Mendota Drive.

3.2 Stop at Eagle Heights Drive; turn left onto bike path.

3.4 Turn left onto path at University Bay Drive.

5.4 Path ends at university student union; turn right onto North Park Street.

5.5 Turn left onto Langdon Street in front of student union.

5.6 Turn right to cross over mall, passing fountain, to base of State Street.

5.7 Continue up State Street to State Capitol.

6.7 Turn right on Carroll Street.

6.8 Turn right onto West Washington Avenue.

7.2 Turn left onto Bassett Street.

7.3 Bassett veers left onto Wilson Street.

7.5 Turn right onto Broom Street.

7.6 Turn right onto John Nolen Drive.

7.7 Turn right onto North Shore Drive.

7.8 At Bedford Street, cross over North Shore Drive to bike path around Monona Bay; follow path.

8.6 Path ends; go left onto West Shore Drive.

8.9 Turn right onto paved path.

9.0 Cross South Park Street; go straight on Heywood Drive.

9.2 Cross Wingra Drive; go straight onto Arboretum Drive.

11.4 Continue straight past barricades.

12.2 Turn right onto Seminole Highway.

12.3 Turn right onto Manitou Way.

12.9 Turn right onto Nakoma Road.

13.2  Nakoma Road flows into Monroe Street.
13.3  Turn left onto Glenway Street.
13.9  Turn left onto Mineral Point Road.
14.4  Turn right onto Owen Drive.
14.9  Turn left onto Regent Street.
15.8  Continue on Regent Street to Eau Claire Street, at Renne-
       bohn Park.

---

for the swimming pool across Eau Claire from the park. Head north on Eau Claire. After crossing Sheboygan and coming to Old Middleton Road at four-tenths of a mile, cross over to the sidewalk and bike path that leads to the left under the highway. Cross the railroad tracks and come out at a small park. Follow the path to the right around the park and pedal up Merrill Springs Road through a quiet, well-kept residential area.

At 1 mile turn right onto Lake Mendota Drive along the shore of Lake Mendota through a rustic urban area of heavily forested roads past a golf course to the right. You'll find it hard to believe that you're in a major city. Stop at Eagle Heights Drive at 3.2 miles and turn left down a bike path. A quarter of a mile later, this will come out at University Bay Drive and another bike path along the lake; follow the path as it cuts in along Lake Mendota's shore, with the university to the right. The path changes from asphalt to hard-packed dirt through a forested area, with the lake immediately to the left. At 5.2 miles stay right around the building directly ahead to the University Student Union and at 5.4 miles, the end of the path. Turn right here onto North Park Street, go one block to a left on Langdon, and pass in front of the Union. To your right will be a small mall with a fountain in the middle; cross the mall, and you'll be at the base of State Street, with the State Capitol on the hill above.

State Street is the bustling heart of Madison, with unique shops, restaurants, bars, and bookstores along with wandering musicians, street people, burned-out hippies, students, skin heads, Day-Glo mohawk haircuts, preachers, and politicians. Only service vehicles are allowed on State Street, so, as a bicyclist or pedestrian, you have it to yourself.

Be sure to lock your bike securely if you stop to eat, browse, or visit the Capitol building; although Madison is a bike-friendly city, thieves are drawn to a university town with lots of bikes. Be aware.

At the Capitol, 6.7 miles, turn right onto Carroll Street; then take the next right onto West Washington Avenue. At 7.2 miles turn left onto Bassett Street, which will veer left into Wilson Street. Turn right onto Broom Street at 7.5 miles, then right onto John Nolen Drive at the stoplights. This is a busy road, but you'll be on it for less than a block. Turn right again onto the very next street, North Shore Drive, at 7.7 miles. As you approach Monona Bay ahead, cross over and get on the bike path that circles the bay. Follow this until the path runs out at West Shore Drive, 8.6 miles. Go left on West Shore to 8.9 miles. On the right will be a TWO HOUR PARKING sign, where you'll see a concrete path that leads over to the next street. Cross over on this one block to South Park Street. Cross Park and continue up Heywood Drive. Stop at 9.2 miles, cross Wingra Drive, and enter the University Arboretum on Arboretum Drive (also known as McCafferty Drive).

Be prepared to be transported into another part of the state: Arboretum Drive winds through a dense forest, passing the cattails along the shore of Lake Wingra, and leads back into the forest. It's hard to believe that this absolutely incredible ride exists in the heart of the city. The only difference between riding here and in the secluded Northwoods is the people: You will not be alone in the arboretum, as it is popular with runners, other cyclists, walkers, and car cruisers.

At 11.4 miles you'll come to barricades that force cars to turn back; cyclists, however, can continue as the road weaves and winds through more forest. At 12.2 miles turn right onto Seminole Highway; then make an immediate right onto Manitou

Way, with a park and golf course to your right. Turn right onto Nakoma Road at 12.9 miles and stay with it as it flows into Monroe Street at 13.2 miles.

Turn right onto Glenway Road at 13.3 miles and climb a stiff uphill. Turn left onto Mineral Point Road at 13.9 miles with a bit more uphill. At Owen Drive, 14.4 miles, turn right for a good half-mile-long downhill. Unfortunately, the road surface, cross streets, and a stop sign at Regent Street force you to ride the brakes all the way. Use caution on this hill. Turn left onto Regent Street and ride back to Eau Claire Street at 15.8 miles.

# **Mount Horeb Mound Bounding**

| | |
|---|---|
| **Number of miles:** | 19.6 |
| **Approximate pedaling time:** | 2.5 hours |
| **Terrain:** | Rolling, with some challenging hills |
| **Traffic:** | Light |
| **Things to see:** | Small towns of Mount Horeb and Blue Mounds, Mustard Museum, Blue Mound State Park and Cave of the Mounds nearby, scenic valleys, rural countryside |
| **Food:** | Mount Horeb; Blue Mounds at 15.1 miles |

I had intended this ride to start and end at Blue Mound State Park, just north of the small town of Blue Mounds. At 1,716 feet, the park is the highest point in southern Wisconsin, and the road up to the park is an evil climb for bicyclists. While working my way very slowly to the park entrance, I decided that Blue Mound State Park would not officially be part of this ride. There are hills enough in southern Wisconsin without having to ride this particular one.

That isn't to say that cyclists should avoid Blue Mound State Park. To the contrary, if you have the legs for it, take a ride up (or drive up after your ride!) to the state park. Three-quarters of the way through this ride you'll be at the southern end of the town of Blue Mounds, just below the park. Viewed from a distance, this bluish-gray mound is an impressive site. Close up, the sites seen from it are even more impressive. The park has 40-foot observation towers, but viewing at numerous ground-level

locations is almost as nice. You can easily see the rolling hills of the Wisconsin River watershed, the distant hills of the Baraboo Range, and several other large mounds.

The ride begins to the east of Blue Mounds at a city park in Mount Horeb, three-tenths of a mile south of County ID on Bluemound Street. Mount Horeb sits on a ridge overlooking the rich agricultural land that first brought Swiss and Norwegian settlers to the area. Visit the Hoff Mall (a former turn-of-the-century department store, now specialty shops), several antiques malls, or, if you like mustards, there's the Mount Horeb Mustard Museum on Main Street, with more than 2,000 different mustards. You can even sample a few.

Head left (south) from the park downhill as the road narrows and passes beneath the highway. At around seven-tenths of a mile it becomes Sand Rock Road and, following a hilly stretch, flattens out a bit into a valley before a right turn at 2.1 miles onto Barton Road.

Cross a stream and follow the curvy road uphill, then through some rolling terrain. At 2.8 miles turn left onto East Blue Mound Road, although there's no sign here to help you out. Just take the next left after turning onto Barton.

Here you'll ride a ridge through farm fields, with good views of the rolling countryside. The road twists and rolls, but there are no steep hills in this section. At 4.7 miles continue straight as East Blue Mound blends into Blue Valley Road; do not take the hard right turn. You'll be on the right road if you cross a stream at 4.8 miles. Blue Valley Road flattens out a little as it passes through farm fields. It then climbs at around 5.5 miles, followed by a drop into a scenic valley and a slight uphill to the intersection with Highway 78 at 6.6 miles.

Turn right onto 78, where you'll be high up on a ridge, with spectacular panoramic views in all directions. At 7 miles turn left onto Mayflower Road and enjoy a nice downhill run into a beautiful valley. Stop at 9 miles and turn left onto County E. There's no sign here, but it's the only stop you'll make on Mayflower Road.

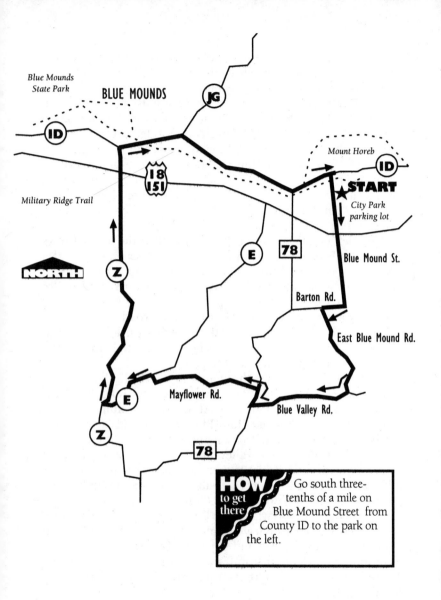

Blue Mounds
State Park

BLUE MOUNDS

JG

ID

Mount Horeb

ID

Military Ridge Trail

18
151

★ START

City Park
parking lot

NORTH

Z

E

78

Blue Mound St.

Barton Rd.

East Blue Mound Rd.

E

Mayflower Rd.

Z

Blue Valley Rd.

78

**HOW**
to get
there

Go south three-
tenths of a mile on
Blue Mound Street from
County ID to the park on
the left.

**DIREC- TIONS at a glance**

| | |
|---|---|
| 0.0 | Turn left from the parking lot onto Blue Mound Street. |
| 2.1 | Turn right onto Barton Road. |
| 2.8 | Turn left onto East Blue Mound Road (the first possible turn; no sign). |
| 4.7 | Continue straight onto Blue Valley Road. |
| 4.8 | Cross stream. |
| 6.6 | Turn right onto Highway 78. |
| 7.0 | Turn left onto Mayflower Road. |
| 9.0 | Turn left onto County E (the first possible turn; no sign). |
| 10.2 | Turn right onto County Z. |
| 14.8 | Cross Highway 18/151. |
| 15.1 | Turn right onto County ID or Military Ridge Trail. |
| 16.5 | Continue past County JG to the left. |
| 19.3 | Turn right onto Blue Mound Street. |
| 19.6 | Return to park. |

Follow the twisting road to a stop at County Z and turn right. The road zigzags back and forth, crossing a few streams before a fairly stiff climb from 13 to 13.5 miles. A downhill takes you toward the town of Blue Mounds ahead. At 14.8 miles stop; then cross Highway 18/151 to a stop at County ID at 15.1 miles. Blue Mound State Park is 2 miles to the northwest.

There are two choices here: Either ride County ID back to Mount Horeb or access the Military Ridge Trail. Military Ridge is a crushed-limestone-surface rail-trail that runs from 39.6 miles between Verona to the east and Dodgeville to the west. The trail lies on a ridge separating the streams that flow north to the Wisconsin River and south to the Mississippi. Established as a crude roadway between Green Bay and Prairie du Chien in the mid-1800s, a railroad was built along this portion of the ridge in 1880–81. The trail has the advantage of no traffic, but County ID has a paved surface; the distance back to the park is the same. Cave of the Mounds is about 1 mile north of County ID off County F. A large limestone cavern discovered in 1939, it's one of the more significant known caves in the Midwest.

County ID is mostly flat on its way back into Mount Horeb; the Military Ridge Trail runs parallel to the road. At 19.3 miles turn right onto Blue Mound Street, and you're back at the park at 19.6 miles.

# A Wright-Stuff Ride

| | |
|---:|:---|
| **Number of miles:** | 19.7 |
| **Approximate pedaling time:** | 2.5 hours |
| **Terrain:** | Rolling, with some challenging hills |
| **Traffic:** | Light throughout except for moderate on Highway 23 |
| **Things to see:** | Wisconsin River, Tower Hill State Park, Frank Lloyd Wright Visitor Center, Frank Lloyd Wright home, American Players Theatre, scenic valleys |
| **Food:** | Water at the park; Hyde at 10.1 miles |

Spring Green is synonymous with famed architect Frank Lloyd Wright, who was born 18 miles to the north in Richland Center. As a child, Wright spent much of his time in the Spring Green area, which was settled by his Welsh ancestors in the mid-1800s. He spent the last forty-eight years of his life at Taliesin (Welsh for "Shining Brow"), the home and estate he designed and built for himself. You'll see Taliesin at the end of the ride and pass by the Frank Lloyd Wright Visitor Center on the way to the start. On a visit to the 600-acre Taliesin complex, you'll see five Wright-designed buildings.

The ride begins at Tower Hill State Park, where lead shot was made during the mid-1800s along the high bluffs of the Wisconsin River. Here melted lead was dropped from ladles down a 180-foot shaft into a pool of water. As the lead fell and cooled, it formed into reasonably round pellets of shot. A portion of the shot tower and the smelter house have been rebuilt; the park offers a video program and displays that show how the shot was made.

From the park entrance turn right on County C to the next left, a tenth of a mile, onto Golf Course Road. Within less than a mile, you'll pass the Springs Golf Club Resort on the right and the award-winning American Players Theatre on the left. APT is devoted exclusively to the classics, and all productions are staged in an outdoor amphitheater, with the dense Wisconsin River Valley forest as a backdrop.

This is hilly country, so be prepared for some slow, grinding uphills and fast downhills. The stunning scenery of the rolling hills and valleys makes the ride worth it, however. You'll use your lowest gear for the first mile before coming to a stop at 1.5 miles and a right turn. There's no sign here, but it used to be Tower Hill Road. You'll climb again, up and away from the Wisconsin River, then negotiate the first of several zigzag drops. Be careful because there's a sharp left to be negotiated at 2.5 miles, then a swing to the right. It's a great, primarily downhill run.

At 3.4 miles stop and turn right onto High Point Road. After weaving back and forth as the road picks its way through hills, a gradual uphill grade begins around 4 miles as you continue right onto Coon Rock Road. Turn left onto Amacher Hollow Road at 4.3 miles, climb a small hill, then begin a drop down into the hollow. Control your speed for a bend to the left at 4.7 miles along this gorgeous run, as you'll pop up and down over small hills to another very nice drop at 6.5 miles.

After crossing a stream, stop at County H and turn right at 7.1 miles. There's no road sign here. Ride down through the hollow on a reasonably level stretch of road through open farm fields. The ups and downs begin around 8 miles and continue as County H blends into County T. County T goes both left and right here; stay to the right and go right again on T at 10.1 miles. Go straight for less than a mile to the small community of Hyde for a rest stop.

County T follows along a hillside, curving left and right, with a valley below. The grade picks up at 12 miles and continues more up than down for another mile. At 13.5 miles you'll swing to the right on a nice downhill, then back to the left

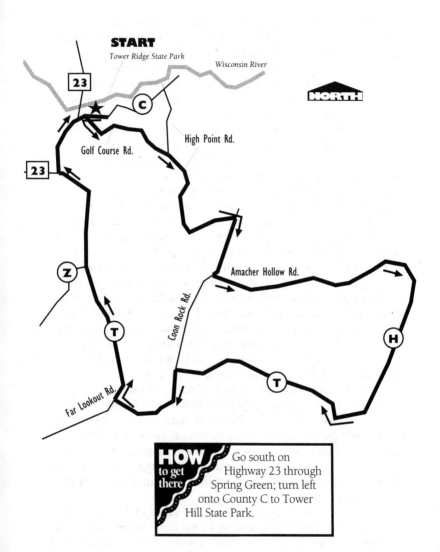

START

Tower Ridge State Park

Wisconsin River

NORTH

23

C

Golf Course Rd.

High Point Rd.

23

Amacher Hollow Rd.

Z

Coon Rock Rd.

T

H

T

Far Lookout Rd.

**HOW** to get there
Go south on Highway 23 through Spring Green; turn left onto County C to Tower Hill State Park.

**DIREC-TIONS at a glance**

| | |
|---|---|
| 0.0 | From Tower Ridge State Park, turn right onto County C. |
| 0.1 | Turn left onto Golf Course Road. |
| 1.5 | Turn right at first intersection (no sign; formerly Tower Hill Road). |
| 3.4 | Turn right onto High Point Road. |
| 4.0 | Continue right onto Coon Rock Road. |
| 4.3 | Turn left onto Amacher Hollow Road. |
| 7.1 | Turn right onto County H (no sign). |
| 9.9 | Turn right onto County T. |
| 10.1 | Turn right again onto County T. |
| 13.1 | Continue past Coon Rock Road. |
| 14.3 | Continue past Far Lookout Road. |
| 16.5 | Continue past County Z. |
| 18.2 | Turn right onto Highway 23. |
| 18.9 | Turn right onto County C. |
| 19.7 | Return to park. |

sharply, so watch your speed. After cresting a knob, there's yet another spectacular downhill run at 14 miles, followed by a winding ride through a tight valley.

This is a very pretty section, with small fields to the right and hills rising all around. The road, which follows the hillside and the lay of the land, opens up at 16.5 miles into another small valley and gently swoops to the left at 17.5 miles.

As you approach Highway 23 at 18.2 miles, the unmistakable architecture of Frank Lloyd Wright is on the hillside across the highway; that's Taliesin. The entrance is to the left. Turn right onto Highway 23 to County C at 18.2 miles. The Frank Lloyd Wright Visitor Center is on the right at 18.9 miles. The ride back to the park is mostly uphill from here, with a turnout to view the Wisconsin River at 19.3 miles. At 19.7 miles you're back at the park entrance.

# Ocooch Mountain Climb

| | |
|---:|:---|
| Number of miles: | 15.4 |
| Approximate pedaling time: | 2 hours |
| Terrain: | Rolling, with several challenging hills |
| Traffic: | Light, except on Highway 80 coming back into town |
| Things to see: | Richland Center, orchards, valleys, and panoramic views |
| Food: | In Richland Center |

No, there are no true mountains in Wisconsin anymore, but once upon a time, there were mountains to rival those paltry hills out west. To find them, you have to travel back in time millions and millions of years. What remains, after several Ice Age episodes, are some hills that make you think you're in mountains when you're riding a bike. These hills and ridgetops are known locally as the Ocooch Mountains.

Although hilly countryside surrounds Richland Center, the Ocooch Fall Bicycle Tour, one of Wisconsin's most scenic rides, uses the roads of this ride for one of its short and less challenging loops. Hills are unavoidable here, but there are only a couple of true gut-wrenchers.

From the University of Wisconsin–Richland Center parking lot, head straight across Highway 14 to West Side Drive, a residential street. Start out climbing a small hill, with Richland Center down below to your left. Stay to the right past Steward Street, which would take you into the city. West Side Drive merges into Grove Street at six-tenths of a mile. Go downhill to a right turn on Seminary Street at eight-tenths of a mile.

Heading away from town, turn left onto County Y at 1.1

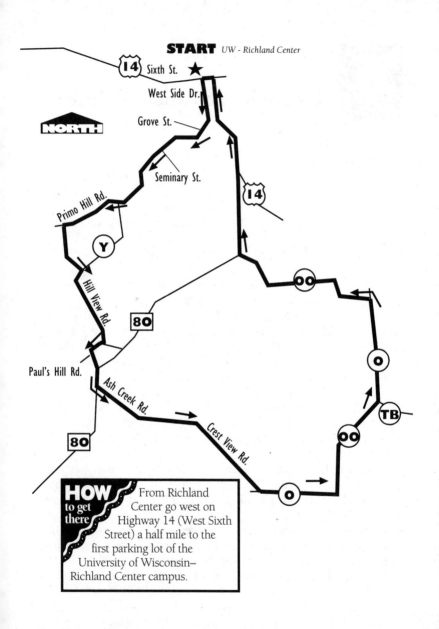

**START** *UW - Richland Center*

(14) Sixth St.

West Side Dr.

Grove St.

Seminary St.

Primo Hill Rd.

(14)

(Y)

Hill View Rd.

(80)

Paul's Hill Rd.

Ash Creek Rd.

Crest View Rd.

(80)

**HOW** to get there — From Richland Center go west on Highway 14 (West Sixth Street) a half mile to the first parking lot of the University of Wisconsin–Richland Center campus.

**NORTH**

**DIREC- TIONS at a glance**

| | |
|---|---|
| 0.0 | Cross Highway 14 to West Side Drive. |
| 0.6 | Continue to the right on Grove Street. |
| 0.8 | Turn right onto Seminary Street. |
| 1.1 | Turn left onto County Y. |
| 2.1 | Turn right onto Primo Hill Road. |
| 2.8 | Turn left onto Hill View Road. |
| 3.4 | Turn right onto County Y. |
| 3.5 | Continue straight onto Hill View Road. |
| 4.3 | Turn right onto Paul's Hill Road. |
| 4.9 | Turn right onto Highway 80. |
| 5.0 | Turn left onto Ash Creek Road. |
| 6.5 | Continue straight onto Crest View Drive. |
| 7.7 | Turn left onto County O. |
| 8.5 | Turn left at County O/County OO. |
| 9.8 | Continue past County TB. |
| 11.0 | Turn left onto County OO. |
| 12.8 | Turn right, continuing on County OO. |
| 13.3 | Turn right onto West Fourteenth Street (Highway 80). |
| 14.3 | Continue straight. |
| 14.9 | Turn left onto Sixth Street (Highway 14). |
| 15.4 | Return to University of Wisconsin Richland Center parking lot. |

miles. A hilly golf course with a stream meandering through it is off to the left as you pedal up County Y. The road begins to wind downhill, with rugged hills on both sides. Stay to the right at 2.1 miles, where County Y turns left, on Primo Hill Road. Primo Hill Road is hilly with a fairly steady, long, winding climb, although you might not choose the word *primo* for this road. In fact, I passed another cyclist who chose to walk the last few hundred yards of this half-mile adventure. The Ocooch area is known for its orchards, which you'll pass on the left after climbing Primo Hill.

Turn left onto Hill View Road at 2.8 miles and get a view of the hill you'll be climbing right up ahead. Crest the hill at 3.2 miles, pass through a quaint farm, and swing to the left, then right, around an apple orchard. Right before the intersection with County Y, you might encounter a small stretch of gravel, although it likely will be paved over.

At 3.4 miles Hill View joins County Y with a right turn; then Hill View continues straight as Y goes to the right. After climbing a little you'll feel as though you've scaled to the top of the Ocooch Mountains, but you'll be rewarded with an outstanding panoramic view. Take a drink from your water bottle, enjoy this spectacularly scenic spot, and then sit back for a wonderful downhill through rolling farm fields, with tree-lined ridges off in the distance. At 3.8 miles you pass, literally, through a farm; watch your speed, as there might be some farm "droppings" on the road. At 4.1 miles there's a tight turn to left before a stop at 4.3 miles and a right turn on Paul's Hill Road.

The road continues its plunge down into a valley. Keep your hands on your brakes, as you'll pick up a lot a speed, and swing to the left at the bottom, right before the stop sign at Highway 80. Turn right, then left almost immediately onto Ash Creek Road.

Ash Creek Road is carved into a hillside, with a valley below. There aren't a lot of terrain changes as the road works its way down into the valley and along Ash Creek. Hills rise up on both sides of the road as you pass small farms on the way to a wider valley after 6 miles. At 6.5 miles stay to the right onto Crest View Drive and continue through the valley. You pass through a small wetland and then come up to a stop at County O.

County O has more roll to it as the gorgeous valley views continue. At 8.5 miles turn left at County O/County OO and follow along as the road curves gently to the right. At 9.8 miles pass County TB, which goes off to the right. The hills become more challenging as the roller-coaster effect picks up. There are no steep climbs, however. Just after 10 miles let loose on a nice, straight downhill.

Turn left onto County OO at 11 miles; County O goes

straight ahead here. The road veers left and right, with a few climbs, as you stay with the valley-riding theme. Pass a huge farm to the right at 11.6 miles, then face a decent climb as the road swings to the right at 12.2 miles, followed by a downhill run with a sweeping turn to the left. Stop and turn right at 12.8 miles, staying on County OO.

Cross a bridge and come back into the Richland Center residential area. Turn right onto West Fourteenth Street (Highway 80), a four-lane road. Stay to the right, following the highway into town. Continue past County Q and County N at 14.3 miles in the heart of Richland Center. If the bustle of the traffic in this town (population 5,000) bothers you, ride a parallel street up to Sixth Street (Highway 14) and turn left. Pass the high school on the right, cross the bridge, and return to the parking lot at 15.4 miles.

# Amish Country Amble

| | |
|---:|:---|
| Number of miles: | 20.5 |
| Approximate pedaling time: | 2.5 hours |
| Terrain: | Hilly |
| Traffic: | Light |
| Things to see: | Cashton, Amish farms, scenic Coulee valleys, cheese factory |
| Food: | Cashton; 2.2 miles, Peck's Bar and Grill; 15.5 miles, Hill and Valley Cheese; 17.8 miles, Peck's Bar and Grill |

Cashton is a pretty, small farm town that is definitely not on the beaten tourist track, which makes it all the better for a bike ride. Cashton is also in the hilly Coulee Country, which makes it a challenging ride, the first half of which is a lot of downhill and the second half a lot of uphill.

Begin at Cashton Park off Highway 33 at the western edge of town. Green Street, which leads to the parking lot, is right next to the Cashton Veterans' Memorial. From the parking lot turn right onto Front Street (Highway 33) and ride through town, turning right (staying on Highway 33) onto South Street. There's a convenience store at the turn if you need to stock up on any supplies for the ride. Head downhill to the edge of town and turn right onto Oklahoma Road at six-tenths of a mile.

Climb a short but stiff little hill, drop down, and then climb up again—a pattern you'll be very familiar with in the miles to come—into rural farm country. Pass Oclinton Road at 1.4 miles, head down, then face a climb to 1.9 miles. Cross over onto County D and climb some more to 2.2 miles. While this is a

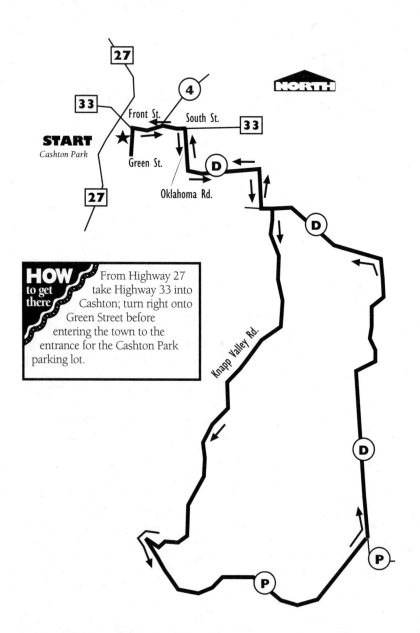

**NORTH**

27

33

4

Front St.

South St.

33

**START**
*Cashton Park*

★

Green St.

Oklahoma Rd.

D

27

D

**HOW**
to get
there

From Highway 27 take Highway 33 into Cashton; turn right onto Green Street before entering the town to the entrance for the Cashton Park parking lot.

Knapp Valley Rd.

D

D

P

P

**DIREC-TIONS** at a glance

0.0 Exit Cashton Park; turn left onto Green Street.

0.1 Turn right onto Front Street (Highway 33).

0.4 Staying on Highway 33, turn right onto South Street.

0.6 Turn right onto Oklahoma Road.

1.9 Continue straight onto County D.

2.2 Continue right on County D.

2.8 Turn right onto Knapp Valley Road.

8.6 Turn left onto County P.

9.1 Continue left on County P at County S.

11.3 County D comes in from the left; continue straight on County P/D.

12.0 County P turns left; continue straight on County D.

14.3 Turn left on County D at Short Cut Road.

17.7 Continue past Knapp Valley Road.

18.6 Continue straight from County D onto Oklahoma Road.

19.9 Turn left onto South Street (Highway 33).

20.1 Turn left onto Front Street (Highway 33).

20.4 Turn left onto Green Street.

20.5 Return to park entrance.

hilly ride, there will be as much down as there is up and only a few long, grinding climbs.

At 2.2 miles County D heads south, with a beautiful view from the top of the ridge before you head down into a 90-degree left turn, with Peck's Bar and Grill on the left. Turn right onto Knapp Valley Road at 2.8 miles.

You'll be on Knapp Valley Road for the next 6.5 miles as it passes between the Clinton Ridge to the right and Wang Ridge to the left, following and occasionally crossing Knapp Creek as it flows into the West Branch of the Kickapoo River. One nice thing about Knapp Valley Road is that it's predominantly downhill. What makes it even better is the spectacular valley scenery.

Drop down into the valley, coasting most of the way to 3.6 miles, where the road hugs the edge of a tight little valley. The road is carved into the hillside at 4.2 miles, with the narrow valley—maybe 100 yards across—down below. The first of several Amish farms comes up on the left at 4.6 miles, easily identified by the blue curtains and lack of power lines running to the house. There's a good chance you'll see a horse-drawn Amish buggy on Knapp Valley Road and, in the right season, see Amish farmers working their rugged fields with a horse-drawn plow.

After crossing a creek and passing a horse farm at 5.5 miles, climb up slightly, hugging the hillside, with the valley staying below. By 6 miles the road continues along the valley floor before heading into a tight tree tunnel and another downhill. The valley opens up a bit as you ride near Knapp Creek, crossing the creek at 8.1 miles and then heading into another valley on the way to County P at 8.6 miles. For much of the next 12 miles, you'll pay the price for the ride down the valley.

Turn left onto County P, cross the creek again, head up to 9.4 miles, drop down to another creek crossing, and then start snaking up again. By 10.3 miles the climb gets steeper as you search for your lowest gear, and it doesn't end until 10.8 miles, the worst of it now behind you. After passing a country church at 11.2 miles, County D comes in from the right and joins County P. Continue straight, up high now with some nice views; then enjoy a good downhill at 11.5 miles. At 12 miles County P turns left; continue straight on County D.

The road weaves left, then right, alternately climbing and dropping, passing several Amish farms and a distinctive round barn on the right at 12.5 miles. From here you can see the series of roller-coaster hills yet to come; let go on the downhills, and your momentum carries you halfway up the next.

There's a nice drop at 14.3 miles but a tight 90-degree turn to the right where Short Cut Road goes straight. At 15.2 miles there's a long, gradual uphill that passes a schoolhouse on the left and Hill and Valley Cheese on the right at 15.9 miles. There's yet another short but grinding uphill after that. Pass several Amish farms at 17.2 miles before a 90-degree turn to the left. Knapp Valley Road is on the left at 11.7 miles.

From here it's a matter of simply retracing the route back to Cashton, climbing the hills you went down before. At 18.6 miles, where County D goes to the right, continue straight on Oklahoma Road to Highway 33 (South Street) at 19.9 miles. Turn left and follow Highway 33 through Cashton back to the park at 20.5 miles.

# Weaving through Wisconsin's Alps

| | |
|---:|:---|
| **Number of miles:** | 27.3 |
| **Approximate pedaling time:** | 3 hours |
| **Terrain:** | Flat to hilly |
| **Traffic:** | Light on county roads; moderate on highways |
| **Things to see:** | Mauston, Lemonweir River, outstanding scenic vistas |
| **Food:** | Mauston |

The Real Wheelin' Bike Race runs out of Mauston each year, billing itself as a ride through the "Alps of Juneau County" into some of Wisconsin's most spectacular scenery. This ride follows that route into the Wisconsin Alps. Mauston is ON THE RIVER OF MEMORIES, as the signs say in town (the river is the Lemonweir), and it sits on I–94 in the center of southern Wisconsin. I never have bothered to ask exactly why the Lemonweir is called the "River of Memories," but I do know that this will be a memorable bike ride.

First, be sure to take plenty of water and whatever food you need for a 27.3-mile, sometimes challenging, ride. If necessary you can take a 1.5-mile detour off County I at 14 miles to head into Wonewoc; just stay on County G to Highway 33.

Actually, this ride is not as grueling as its alpine name suggests, although there a number of stiff climbs and steep descents. The scenery, however, makes the ups and downs well worth it. This ride's sole purpose is to show off the spectacular scenery—no historic sites, no interesting lakes; just mile after mile of picture-postcard views.

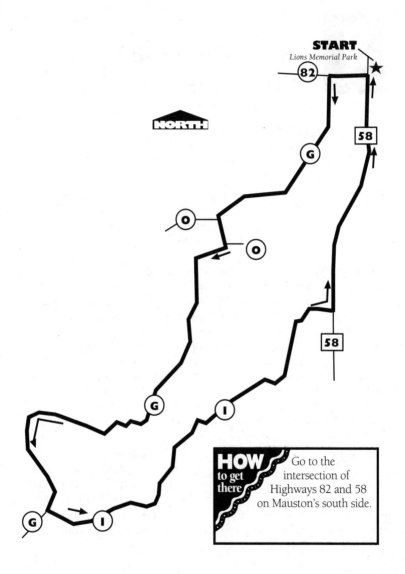

**START**
*Lions Memorial Park*

NORTH

82

58

G

O

O

58

G

I

G

I

**HOW**
**to get**
**there**
Go to the
intersection of
Highways 82 and 58
on Mauston's south side.

**DIREC-TIONS at a glance**

| | |
|---|---|
| 0.0 | From Lions Memorial Park go west on Highway 82. |
| 0.8 | Turn left onto County G. |
| 4.8 | Continue past County O. |
| 5.3 | Continue straight on County G as County O turns left. |
| 14.0 | Turn left onto County I. |
| 22.8 | Turn left onto Highway 58. |
| 27.3 | Return to park. |

Exit the Interstate at Highway 82 and follow that through Mauston to Lions Memorial Park at the junction of Highways 82 and 58 at the south end of town. From the park head west on Highway 82, passing the high school at four-tenths of a mile to a left turn onto County G at eight-tenths of a mile. This is an easy ride for directions: Stay on County G to County I at 14 miles, follow County I to the left until Highway 58 at 22.8 miles, and follow that back to the park.

The first few miles on County G will have you asking, "What Alps?" The road, at first flat through farm fields to a downhill at 1.4 miles, is deceiving; those hills in the distance should give some idea of what's to come. Skirt a ridge at 2.7 miles, and the scenery changes from farm fields to ridges in all directions. The road stays relatively flat and even heads a bit downhill between 3.5 and 4 miles, snaking left and right. Pass a round barn at 4.4 miles and continue straight past County O at 4.8 miles and across One Mile Creek.

A gentle ride up takes you up past a tree-covered ridge on the right. County O goes left at 5.3 miles; stay straight on County G. It's still reasonably flat through here although you'll notice the ridges have moved in closer. At 6 miles the road swings left, and you'll see the first hill. Cross Stewart Creek at

6.5 miles and begin what is at first a gentle climb that soon gets steep. Curve to the right and continue up to a leveling at 7.1 miles, a short drop, and another climb to 7.4 miles that crests finally at 7.8 miles. You're up in the hills now and will stay there for the next 13 to 14 miles.

Drop through a series of rolling hills to a spectacular ridgetop view, at 8.5 miles, of forested hills spilling out in all directions, disturbed only by an occasional farm field. At 9.2 miles use caution as you drop down into a tight turn to the right. Once around the turn you'll straighten out and can enjoy the ride as it bottoms at 10 miles before another climb. Find your lowest gear for the next half mile, after which the grade eases at 10.7 miles, with another wonderful ridgetop view.

One of the best views on the ride comes just before Otts Road at 12.6 miles, where you'll come to understand why the locals call these hills Wisconsin's Alps. The road snakes back and forth across the ridge, coming to a stop at County I, 14 miles. Turn left and then sit back and enjoy a nice downhill into a valley. Ride the brakes as you ease around to the left and cross Gardner Creek at 14.8 miles.

A climb begins here, curving first left, then right, before leveling off at 15.5 miles, followed by another short but steep downhill at 15.7 miles to a stretch of level road that leads to yet another drop at 16.4 miles. Again control your speed as the road takes a sharp left over Crossman Creek.

A short climb at 17.2 miles leads to the edge of forested ridge, where you horseshoe around the ridge with some great views of the valley to the right. Weave along the edge of the ridge without a lot of difficult climbing to a downhill at 20.7, all the while enjoying the scenery off to the right. At 21.8 miles a 90-degree swing to the left is followed by a steep downhill first left, then right, passing through a farm at 22.5 miles. Turn left onto Highway 58 at 22.8 miles.

From here the ride has a few small hills on the way back to Mauston. Just after 25 miles look ahead to see another ridge, but be comforted by the fact that you'll skirt around the worst of it.

Begin to climb over its edge at 25.6 miles to a short, level section before another steady climb to 26.5 miles and a downhill back to Mauston. Pass the Juneau County Fairgrounds at 26.9 miles, and you'll be back at the park at 27.3 miles.

# Tunnel Vision: Elroy-Sparta Trail—and More

| | |
|---:|:---|
| **Number of miles:** | 15.9 |
| **Approximate pedaling time:** | 2 hours |
| **Terrain:** | Flat on the trail, hilly on the road section; one steep, mile-long climb |
| **Traffic:** | Light |
| **Things to see:** | Norwalk, Wilton, Elroy-Sparta Trail, tunnel on the trail, rolling countryside |
| **Food:** | Wilton and Norwalk |

The 32-mile-long Elroy-Sparta Trail is Wisconsin's oldest rail-trail, opened in 1965 on an abandoned railbed, and is one of the country's first rail-trails. Passing through the hilly unglaciated hills and valleys of western Wisconsin, Elroy-Sparta welcomes more than 60,000 visitors each year, many coming for the experience of passing through the trail's three tunnels, the longest of which is three-quarters of a mile.

The tunnels were built in 1873 to allow the Chicago and North Western trains to pass through these rugged Coulee Country hills on no more than a 3-percent grade. The tunnels are dark and damp, a constant 55-or-so degrees during even the hottest summer months. From the middle of Tunnel Three, the entrances are mere pinpricks of light; flashlights are highly recommended not only to guide your way but also to examine the features of the tunnels. For instance, water from an overhead spring cascades down the walls of Tunnel Three. You must walk your bike through the tunnels, by the way.

The problem with rail-trails is that they're always point-to-

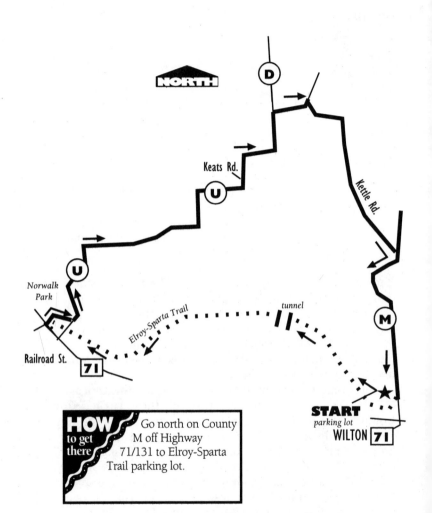

NORTH

D

Keats Rd.

U

Kettle Rd.

U

Norwalk Park

M

Elroy-Sparta Trail

tunnel

Railroad St.

**71**

START
parking lot
WILTON **71**

**HOW** to get there
Go north on County M off Highway 71/131 to Elroy-Sparta Trail parking lot.

**DIREC-TIONS at a glance**

0.0 Enter Elroy-Sparta Trail from the parking lot at Wilton.

2.2 Pass through quarter-mile-long tunnel.

5.7 Norwalk Park; turn right onto Railroad Street.

5.9 Turn left onto County U.

9.9 Turn left onto Keats Road.

11.1 Turn right at County D.

11.7 Turn right onto Kettle Road.

14.2 Turn right onto County M.

15.9 Return to Wilton parking lot.

point; you either have to ride to the end and back again, arrange a shuttle, or loop out onto country roads to your starting point. The trouble with a loop using the Elroy-Sparta Trail has to do with the nature of the trail itself, the reason for digging those tunnels in the first place—this is extremely hilly country.

This ride uses a 5.7-mile section of the trail between Wilton and Norwalk, passing through the quarter-mile-long Tunnel Two, then looping on county roads, first north, then south, and back to Wilton. Start at the Wilton parking lot for the trail and head west on the firmly packed crushed-limestone surface. Be sure to pay before you start out; like all Wisconsin rail-trails, there is a fee to use the trail. Keep an eye on the highway to the left, glimpsed occasionally through the trees, and you'll understand the great feat of engineering it was to keep the trains on no more than a 3-percent grade. The trail is mostly wooded through here, often cut deep into a hill, and the gentle grade is still a noticeable incline. The entrance to the tunnel comes up at 2.2 miles.

Take your time walking through the tunnel, turning your light at the walls and ceiling from time to time. At 2.5 miles you exit the trail and begin a noticeable but gradual downhill. There are several bridge crossings before the trail levels out at around 5 miles. Stop for a road crossing at 5.4 miles just as you enter Norwalk. Continue on past the park to the next stop sign, 5.7 miles, at Railroad Street, although there isn't a sign to indicate the street. Turn left here for one block to head into town for food or drink. To continue the ride, turn right to County U at 5.9 miles.

Follow County U up—and I do mean up—and away from town. This is why there's a flat rail-trail for riding in this area; the climb continues for more than a mile, tapering a bit at 6.8 miles, then continuing up. Once at the top of this hill, however, the rest of the trip isn't too bad as you ride along a ridgetop.

County U takes several sharp 90-degree left and right turns. Pass Kensington Road at 7.4 miles; turn right, staying on County U where Kelton Avenue comes at 8.1 miles; then turn left onto Keats Road at 9.9 miles. Turn right at County D and July Road at 11.1 miles. Views are spectacular from this high country, and the ride down, back to Wilton, is a thrill.

Turn right onto Kettle Road at 11.7 miles, dip down, then back up, with a little valley off to the right. At 12.1 miles there's a sharp turn to the left before the fun really begins; you'll feel as though you're dropping off the top of a mountain, and, in a way, you are. It's very easy to pick up speed on this downhill, so use extreme caution, keeping a firm grip on your brakes, or you'll quickly get out of control. The road flattens out a little at 12.9 miles, then continues down past Kerry Road at 13.5 miles before coming to a stop sign at County M at 14.2 miles.

Turn right and follow County M over a series of small, rolling hills back to the parking lot at 15.9 miles.

# Touring Trempealeau and the Garden of Eden

|  |  |
|---:|:---|
| Number of miles: | 28.3 |
| Approximate pedaling time: | 3.5 hours |
| Terrain: | Rolling, with one challenging, mile-long climb |
| Traffic: | Light |
| Things to see: | Trempealeau, Perot State Park, Mississippi River, Lock and Dam No. 6, Trempealeau National Wildlife Area |
| Food: | Trempealeau; water in Perot State Park; tavern at Pine Creek, 13.9 miles |

According to a local story, an itinerant preacher came upon the hills of what is now Perot State Park and declared he had discovered the biblical Garden of Eden, supporting his argument in a book that called attention to the similarities to the Bible's description of that long-ago paradise. This may not be the Garden of Eden, but locals are prone to call it God's Country, anyway, and with good reason.

Trempealeau is a quaint, old Mississippi River town that is part Mark Twain, part modern tourist center. From the deck of the restored Trempealeau Hotel, Restaurant, and Salon, established in 1871, the Mississippi must look much as it did centuries before European settlers first spied the river. Bluffs tower high above the broad river on both the Wisconsin and Minnesota banks, giving the area a timeless feel.

The ride begins at Trempealeau Sportman's Club/Duck Pond Park. From the parking lot head one block toward the river;

then turn right onto East First Street to Main Street. Continue across Main, with the river to your left, onto West First Street. Don't be surprised to see a train rumble between you and the river. Enter Perot State Park at 1.2 miles, with Ed Sullivan's Restaurant and Supper Club on the left.

The park is an amazing place, rich in the lore of Native Americans and early European settlers. Some of the bluffs in the park rise up more than 500 feet and have been navigational landmarks for centuries. Explorer Nicolas Perot wintered here in 1685–86, and the park is named in his honor. Take some time to explore the park, whether it's just gazing out at the river or climbing the trails to the top of the bluffs.

The heavily forested road through the park is beautiful; it rolls up and down, offering occasional glimpses of the river. A gentle downhill at 2.3 miles drops down next to a river slough, with tall bluffs rising beyond it in the river. The largest of these bluffs is Mount Trempealeau at 384 feet. The French called it *la montagne qui trempe à l'eau,* "the mountain soaking in water." For the Dakotas it was *Pah-hah-dah,* "mountain separated by water." There are more great river views past a parking area at 2.7 miles.

At 3.2 miles a sign points to the park office; continue straight past there to signs pointing to the park exit. As you leave the park, you'll climb up into farm country. Turn left onto Lehmann Road at 3.8 miles and cross the Great River Trail—a limestone-surfaced 14-mile bike trail that leads southeast to La Crosse and northwest to the Trempealeau National Wildlife Refuge.

Turn left at 4.3 miles onto West Prairie Road, with the bluffs of Perot to the left and the Arcadia Ridge in the distance to the right. A long, gradual downhill leads to the entrance of the Wildlife Refuge at 6.9 miles. The roads in the refuge are hard-packed dirt and would be best visited on a mountain bike. Continue past the refuge to a stop at Highway 35/54 at 8 miles. The Arcadia Ridge ahead looks ominous, but you'll have only one tough climb to its top.

Turn left onto Highway 35/54 and travel the narrow paved

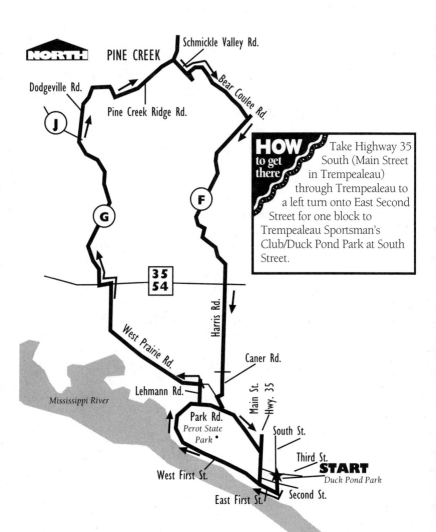

NORTH

PINE CREEK

Schmickle Valley Rd.

Dodgeville Rd.

Bear Coulee Rd.

Pine Creek Ridge Rd.

J

F

G

35 54

**HOW** to get there
Take Highway 35 South (Main Street in Trempealeau) through Trempealeau to a left turn onto East Second Street for one block to Trempealeau Sportsman's Club/Duck Pond Park at South Street.

Harris Rd.

West Prairie Rd.

Caner Rd.

Lehmann Rd.

Mississippi River

Park Rd.
*Perot State Park*

Main St. Hwy. 35

South St.

Third St.

**START**
*Duck Pond Park*

West First St.

Second St.

East First St.

**DIREC-TIONS at a glance**

0.0  From Duck Pond Park, go left for one block on South Street toward the Mississippi River; turn right onto East First Street.

0.2  Continue past Main Street onto West First Street.

1.2  Continue into Perot State Park.

3.2  Continue past sign to park office; follow signs to park exit.

3.8  Turn left onto Lehmann Road.

4.3  Turn left onto West Prairie Road.

8.0  Turn left onto Highway 35/54.

8.4  Turn right onto County G.

11.6  Continue past Whistle Pass Road.

12.3  Continue past County J.

13.7  County G becomes Dodgeville Road.

13.9  Enter the town of Pine Creek.

14.2  Turn right onto Pine Creek Ridge Road.

16.0  Turn right onto Schmickle Valley Road.

16.5  Turn left onto Bear Coulee Road.

18.6  Turn right onto County F.

23.3  Cross Highway 35/54 onto Harris Road.

25.1  Harris Road becomes Caner Road.

25.9  Continue to the right at unmarked T intersection.

26.0  Turn left onto West Prairie Road.

26.3  Turn left onto Park Road.

27.5  Park Road name changes to Pine Street.

28.0  Turn right onto Main Street.

28.2  Turn left onto South Highway 35 (Third Street); go one block and turn right onto South Street.

28.3  Continue on South Street to Second; return to Duck Pond Park.

shoulder to a right at 8.4 miles onto County G. It looks as though you'll have to go right up the ridge, but the road actually skirts the worst of it. At 8.8 miles there's a little downhill that swings around the first ridge for a beautiful view of the valley below. Whistle Pass Road comes in from the right at 11.6 miles, but stay on County G to the left, which opens into a wide valley with a pond down to the left and rolls of ridges beyond.

Continue on County G at 12.3 miles, where County J goes to the left. A nice downhill at 12.8 miles passes right through a farmyard, with buildings on both sides of the road. This entire area has an Appalachian feel to it as you pass through valleys and gaze off at distant ridges.

Stay with County G as it weaves toward Pine Creek and becomes Dodgeville Road as it passes through the town. There's a small tavern to visit for food and refreshments. Coming out of Pine Creek, turn right onto Pine Creek Ridge Road at 14.2 miles. Enjoy the little downhill through the scenic valley because your serious climb begins at 15.1 miles.

This is a mile-long climb, a real grinder that levels briefly halfway up before getting steeper. Once at the top, however, the view is spectacular, and you'll feel as if you're on the top of Wisconsin. Where you are is at the top of the Arcadia Ridge, some 350 feet above sea level. Take a break, enjoy the scenery, and then turn right at 16 miles onto Schmickle Valley Road.

Now you'll be going down the same kind of hill you just came up. Use extreme caution going down; the road is steep, with a lot of twists and turns. Make sure your brakes work and be prepared to use them all the way down. At 16.5 make a sharp left turn, a 180-degree swing onto Bear Coulee Road, and follow this as it twists its way down the ridge. There will be a nice view down into the valley at 16.9 miles.

Turn right onto County F at 18.6 miles and ride through the valley. The terrain is reasonably flat from now on as the road weaves through the valley, passing farm fields. At 23.3 miles cross Highway 35/54 onto Harris Road. Continue past Kribs Road at 25.1 miles, where Harris becomes Caner Road. Stay to the right at the unmarked T intersection at 25.9 miles. Turn left onto West Prairie Road at 26 miles, then left onto Park Road at 26.3 miles. Park Road leads back into town, becoming Pine Street before a stop at Main Street. Turn right, drop into town, and then turn left onto South Highway 35 at 28.2 miles. Go one block and turn right onto South Street to the park at 28.3 miles.

A nice side trip is to Lock and Dam No. 6 on the Mississippi River to see how the huge barges are raised and lowered past the dam. Continue on Second Street away from town. At four-tenths of a mile, Second Street becomes East First Street. Turn right onto Fremont Street at five-tenths of a mile and follow this around to the right to the viewing platform on the river at 1 mile.

# Homage to the Highground

| | |
|---:|:---|
| Number of miles: | 20 |
| Approximate pedaling time: | 2.5 hours |
| Terrain: | Rolling hills |
| Traffic: | Light in the country; moderate on Highway 73 and through town |
| Things to see: | The Highground Veterans Memorial, town of Neillsville, Cheese Pavilion, Black River |
| Food: | In Neillsville, grocery store at 4.5 miles; in Christie, at 9.7 miles |

Neillsville was built around the Black River, which courses through the center of this town of 3,000. Its history can be found at the Jail Museum, in the old jail that was a source of great civic pride when it was built in 1897, operated by the local Historical Society. East of town on Highway 10, have a chat with a cow, Chatty Belle, a much-larger-than-life talking cow stationed next to the Wisconsin Cheese Pavilion—the very same pavilion that represented "America's Dairyland" at the 1964 World's Fair in New York. You're in the very heart of Cheeseland now.

This ride begins at the Highground, a powerful memorial to Wisconsin's veterans. Built on a massive ridge, the Highground overlooks half a million acres of glacial moraine and distant wooded, rolling hills. The Highground began in 1984 as a memorial to Wisconsin's Vietnam veterans and grew to include all Wisconsin veterans. Supported through donations, the Highground is set on one hundred acres, with a large, triangular-

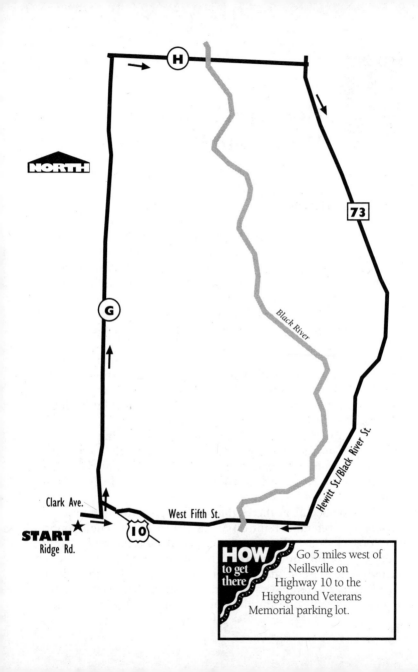

NORTH

H

73

G

Black River

Hewitt St./Black River St.

Clark Ave.

West Fifth St.

**START**
Ridge Rd.

10

**HOW**
to get
there

Go 5 miles west of
Neillsville on
Highway 10 to the
Highground Veterans
Memorial parking lot.

**DIREC-TIONS at a glance**

| | |
|---|---|
| 0.0 | Follow parking-lot road (Ridge Road). |
| 0.3 | Turn left onto Clark Avenue. |
| 0.4 | Cross Highway 10 to County G. |
| 4.5 | Donna and Dave's Grocery Store is on the left. |
| 6.5 | Turn right onto County H. |
| 8.1 | Cross Black River. |
| 9.5 | Turn right onto Highway 73; pass through Christie. |
| 15.7 | Enter Neillsville; Highway 73 becomes Black River Street. |
| 16.2 | Black River Street becomes Hewett Street. |
| 16.4 | Turn right onto West Fifth Street. |
| 17.1 | Cross Black River. |
| 18.7 | Turn right onto Highway 10. |
| 19.6 | Turn left onto Clark Avenue. |
| 19.7 | Turn right onto Ridge Road. |
| 20.0 | Return to parking lot. |

shaped 45,000-square-foot plaza at its center. The memorial includes sculptures that pay tribute to veterans, as well as an earthen effigy mound in the shape of a dove that recognizes prisoners of war and persons missing in action. The Highground is open twenty-four hours a day, every day of the year. The site is lighted in the evening.

From the parking lot ride out on Ridge Road, the entrance road to the east; then turn left turn at Clark Avenue. Cross Highway 10 at four-tenths of a mile and continue straight north onto County G. Easy so far, right? Well, get ready for some Highground Hill Country. This entire ride is a roller coaster of near constant ups and downs through the glaciated countryside.

After crossing Highway 10 look to the ridges off to the left; geologists believe these to be nunataks, hills that actually poked through the glacier and were untouched by the ice sheet that covered much of Wisconsin 10,000 years ago. Pass a Christmas-tree farm on the right before rolling up, then dropping down at a mile and a half; continue up again to 1.8 miles, followed by more rollers to a steeper climb at 2.6 miles—an up-and-down pattern that you'll repeat many times before this ride is over. The good news is that there are few grinding hills—most are of a quarter mile or less.

At 3.6 miles there's a nice little rolling downhill, then rolling climbs to 4.5 miles. Donna and Dave's Grocery Store, in an old barn, sits on the left at 4.8 miles; it will be 5 miles until your next chance for sustenance. The countryside is typical rural Wisconsin—farm fields bordered by an occasional tree line. The hills provide great views to far-distant tree-topped ridges. Look to the left at 5.4 miles for a newer earth-shelter home and to the right just after that for a small, lonely hillside cemetery.

Stop at 6.5 miles for a right turn onto County H and a half-mile-long hill that gets progressively steeper as you ride to its top, followed by a nice downhill through a tree-lined road. Another short climb gives way to a pretty, winding route through trees on the way to a crossing of the Black River at 8.1 miles. Just across the bridge is a gravel parking area on the left where you can stop to check out the river.

A stiff little climb away from the river to 8.5 miles gives a view of rolling hills and ridges across farmland to the left. Another short climb that tops out at 9.5 miles offers an even more impressive view of hills rolling away in all directions. Ride down to a stop at 9.5 miles, turn right onto Highway 73, and pass through the small town of Christie, with a tavern for a food or beverage break. Heading back toward Neillsville, you'll see the ridges you've pedaled around. Despite being a state highway, traffic is not heavy on 73, and there's a small paved shoulder to give you a smooth path to avoid the traffic.

The ride out of Christie is about as flat as it gets on the entire route. Climb a slight hill at 11.4 miles; then drop into another flatter stretch, followed by still more slight downhill. In fact, this section is predominantly down to a bridge crossing Panther Creek, with a short climb from the creek to 13.4 miles. There's a bit more downhill as the highway veers to the right at 13.4 miles, passing County C at 13.7 miles. A gradual uphill begins at 14.2 miles and ends at 14.5 as the road veers left, with another gradual climb to 15 miles and a picture-postcard kind of rural farmland view off to the right.

The Moonlight Supper Club is on the left at 15.2 miles as you enter Neillsville. At 15.7 miles Highway 73 becomes Black River Road through a residential area. Cross the Black River at 16.2 miles and climb up a hill into the center of town. Black River Road has become Hewett Street. Stop at 16.4 miles—there's a gazebo to the left—and turn right onto West Fifth Street. Now the real climbing begins and continues for much of the next 2 miles.

Head west up and out of town to the top of the hill at 16.9 miles. Drop down to another river crossing—it's a good place to gaze up and down the Black River—at 17.1 miles; then climb again. The road levels out a bit at 17.8 miles, crests at 18.1 miles, drops down briefly, and then climbs again to 18.6 miles. Turn right onto Highway 10 at 18.7 miles and climb some more to 19.1 miles. There's a good view of distant ridges off to the left At 19.6 miles turn right, following the signs back to the High ground parking lot at 20 miles.

# Red Cedar Ramble

| | |
|---:|:---|
| Number of miles: | 18 |
| Approximate pedaling time: | 2 hours |
| Terrain: | Flat on the trail; some steep hills in the 5 miles after leaving the trail, then moderate |
| Traffic: | Light |
| Things to see: | City of Menomonie, University of Wisconsin–Stout, Red Cedar Trail, Riverside Park, Mabel Tainter Memorial Museum, Wilson Place Museum, Dunn County Heritage Center, Lions Club Game Park |
| Food: | In Menomonie; in Downsville, at 7.7 miles |

In the early 1800s the pine forests of the Red Cedar Valley brought the lumber barons to what would later be Dunn County. By 1888 a railroad line was built along the banks of the Red Cedar River to serve one of the largest white-pine milling companies in the world. Of course, trees are not an unlimited resource; by the early 1900s the forests were depleted, and the logging era came to an end. At present bicyclists can enjoy what's left of that era by riding on the Red Cedar Trail, constructed on the railbed along the banks of the Red Cedar River.

The ride begins at Riverside Park in Menomonie, home to the University of Wisconsin–Stout. To find out more about the lumber days, visit the Wilson Place Museum on First Street, furnished with the belongings of three generations of lumber-baron families and containing exhibits about the area's past. More his-

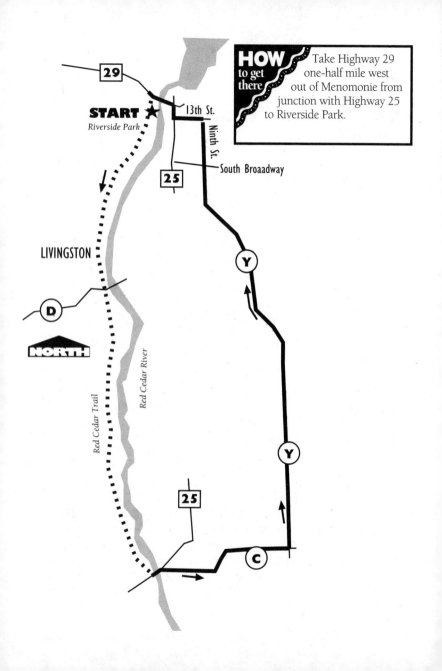

HOW to get there

Take Highway 29 one-half mile west out of Menomonie from junction with Highway 25 to Riverside Park.

29

START
Riverside Park

13th St.

Ninth St.

25

South Broaadway

Y

Y

LIVINGSTON

D

NORTH

Red Cedar Trail

Red Cedar River

25

C

0.0 At Riverside Park, go onto Red Cedar Trail.
2.9 Pass the village of Livingston trail access.
7.7 Leave trail; cross Highway 25 onto County C.
10.0 Turn left onto County Y.
16.0 County Y becomes Ninth Street.
16.8 Turn left onto Thirteenth Street.
17.3 Turn right onto South Broadway (Highway 25).
17.4 Turn left onto Highway 29.
17.9 Cross Red Cedar River.
18.0 Return to Riverside Park entrance.

tory can be found at the Dunn County Historical Society Heritage Center, on the corner of Seventh and Wilson. Built in 1889, the Mabel Tainter Memorial Theater, on Main Street, has been beautifully restored. At Wakanda Park, just north of the city, youngsters might enjoy a visit to the Lions Club Game Park, with deer, elk, and buffalo.

Access the Red Cedar Trail adjacent to Riverside Park. There's a daily fee to ride the trail, or you can purchase an annual pass that is good at all state trails. The trail—with a hard-packed, crushed-limestone surface—follows  the banks of the river first through a tunnel of trees. A bench at 1 mile allows you to have a seat while gazing out at the gently flowing river. For the next mile a high, tree-covered embankment rises up on the right as the trail hugs the river. The lack of development along this stretch of river gives the ride a wilderness feel.

After 2 miles the scenery opens up to the right, offering a view of high rolling hills in the distance, making you thankful for the engineers who provided the nearly level grade of the trail. A parking lot and trail access for the small town of Livingston comes in on the right at 3 miles. Pass under County D; then ride along another section with a high embankment on the right. A few houses appear across the river, the first development since leaving Menomonie.

At 3.4 miles the trail swings away from the river into a more heavily forested area, then through a marshy wetland before coming back through the trees to the river at 4.7 miles. The trail will wander away from the river then back again several times in the next few miles. At 5 miles pass through another area where the original railbed was cut through a steep hill next to the river, ride through a short tunnel of trees (there are picnic tables at 6 miles), and then break out into an open area at 6.7 miles, where there's a cornfield next to the trail.

Enter a pleasant forest at 7 miles, cross the river on a long bridge at 7.2 miles, and continue to Highway 25. Either stay to the left and head straight across the highway, passing a barricade, or swing down to the right and under the bridge; either way will get you into Downsville.

Downsville is a bustling little biker berg that caters to cyclists; you'll find shops, restaurants, inns, and taverns. By 8 miles you're through town and heading uphill. The next 5 miles will be quite different from the flat trail. Slip into your lowest gear and grind up for a half mile into rolling farm country. At 8.8 miles the road swings 90 degrees to the left, with a slight incline after the turn, then 90 degrees to the right with a short but steep climb. Drop down momentarily; then ride a steady but not too steep grade up to 9.5 miles.

Turn left onto County Y at 10 miles and swoop down to enjoy the scenic vistas ahead and off to the left—a patchwork quilt of farm fields and distant forested hills. The road follows a pattern of short roller-coaster hills, quick little drops with short but fairly steep climbs, to begin the process all over again. At 330th/Valley View Road, 11.5 miles, there's an excellent view of the countryside before a nice downhill run.

By 12 miles the worst of the climbing is behind you, although what's to come is by no means flat. At 13.3 miles begin a slight climb to a sharp left at 13.5 miles, where 410th/Hilltop Road comes in from the right. At 13.7 miles stay right onto

County Y through a small valley that leads through a cluster of residences. At 14.6 climb slightly into another valley to a gentle downhill back into Menomonie.

Just after 16 miles County Y becomes Ninth Street. There's a small shopping center and a mini-mart at 16.7 before a left turn onto Thirteenth Street at 16.8 miles, which drops down through the University of Wisconsin–Stout campus. At 17.3 miles turn right onto South Broadway (there's a Dairy Queen at the corner) and go two blocks north; then turn left onto Highway 29, drop down across the river, and, at 18 miles, you're back at Riverside Park.

# Chippin' Away at Lake Wissota

| | |
|---|---|
| Number of miles: | 25 |
| Approximate pedaling time: | 3 hours |
| Terrain: | Flat to rolling |
| Traffic: | Light in the country; moderate through Chippewa Falls |
| Things to see: | Chippewa Falls, Chippewa River, Lake Wissota, Lake Wissota State Park, Leinenkugels Brewery, Irvine Park |
| Food: | In Chippewa Falls; restaurant at 4.9 miles; several restaurants at 19.5 miles |

After reading through the directions for this ride, you might be tempted to skip it, thinking you'll get lost on all the turns. Trust me—it's a lot easier to ride than it is to write; it's just that every time there's a turn in the road, it seems there's a name change, and, for accuracy's sake, I listed them all. Many of the "turns" are nothing more than a no-choice left or right, and with each turn there's a new road name. Maybe the county budget had a little money left over one year, and it was decided to use the money for street signs. Anyway, the route is not difficult to follow, and it is a very rewarding ride.

Start at Irvine Park in Chippewa Falls, and save a little time either before or after the ride to explore this huge park. There's a zoo, playgrounds, swimming pool, hiking trails, and camping. Just down the street from the park—you'll pass it right before the ride ends—is one of America's finest small breweries,

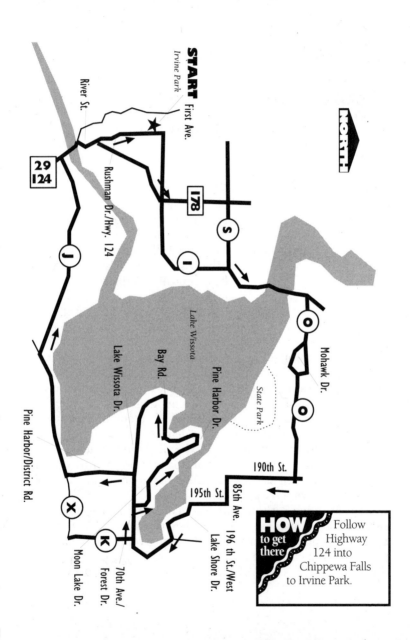

**DIREC-TIONS at a glance**

| | |
|---|---|
| 0.0 | Turn left onto Jefferson Avenue from Irvine Park parking lot. |
| 0.4 | Turn right onto First Avenue. |
| 1.6 | Turn right onto Halbleib Road. |
| 1.7 | Turn left onto Kennedy Road. |
| 1.8 | Turn right onto County I. |
| 1.9 | Cross Highway 178. |
| 3.8 | Turn right onto County S. |
| 5.1 | Turn right onto County O. |
| 5.9 | Turn right onto Mohawk Drive/171st St. |
| 6.5 | Turn right onto County O. |
| 7.1 | Continue past Lake Wissota State Park entrance. |
| 8.0 | Turn right onto 190th Street. |
| 8.9 | Turn left onto 85th Avenue. |
| 9.4 | Turn right onto 195th Street. |
| 10.0 | Turn right onto 196th Street/West Lake Shore Drive. |
| 10.7 | West Lake Shore Drive becomes 75th Avenue. |
| 11.0 | Turn right onto County K. |
| 11.9 | Continue straight onto 70th Street/Forest Drive. |
| 12.2 | Turn right onto 74th Avenue/Moon Lake Drive. |
| 13.4 | Continue onto 76th Avenue (name changes)/ Moon Lake Drive. |
| 13.7 | Turn right onto 78th Avenue/Pine Harbor Drive. |
| 14.1 | Continue straight on Pine Harbor Drive, now 79th Street. |
| 14.4 | Continue on Pine Harbor Drive, now 183rd Street. |
| 15.2 | Turn right onto 75th Avenue/Bay Road. |
| 16.0 | Turn left onto 178th Street/Lake Wissota Drive. |
| 17.5 | Turn right onto 190th Street/Pine Harbor District Road |
| 18.2 | Turn right onto County X. |
| 20.3 | Turn right onto County J. |
| 23.4 | Turn right onto Highway 29/124. |
| 24.0 | Turn right onto River Street East, Highway 124/178. |
| 24.1 | Continue left on Rushman Street (name changes), Highway 124/178. |

**24.3** Continue straight on Highway 124/Rushman Street.
**25.0** Return to park entrance to the left.

---

Leinenkugel's, with tours, a museum, and a hospitality room. On West Grand Avenue the 1873 Cook-Rutledge Mansion, the restored home of one of the area's early lumber barons, is open for tours.

Park in one of the first lots and exit left onto Jefferson Street. Pass the YMCA on the right; then turn right onto First Avenue at four-tenths of a mile. From here the easiest thing to do is follow the blue-and-white HOSPITAL signs, as the route goes through residential areas and past the industrial park on the way to Lake Wissota. Following the hospital signs, turn right onto Halbleib Road at 1.6 miles, left onto Kennedy Road at 1.7 miles, and then right onto County I at 1.8 miles before a stop at Highway 178. Cross the highway on County I and then pass the hospital on the right.

At 2.7 miles the road will veer left and offer the first glimpse of Lake Wissota, a huge lake created by a dam on the Chippewa River in 1918. Turn right onto County S at 3.8 miles and then cross a wide bridge across the west end of the lake at 4.5 miles. There's a restaurant just across the bridge. Turn right onto County O at 5.1 miles (follow the signs to Lake Wissota State Park). Turn right onto Mohawk Drive at 5.9 miles for a ride closer to the lake through an area with some lakefront homes. Don't worry if you miss it; at 6.5 miles it comes back to County O, a right turn.

Pass an ostrich farm on the left at 6.9 miles just before the entrance to Lake Wissota State Park on the left. If you have the time, ride back into the park on several miles of paved roads. There are also 12 miles of hiking trails, as well as camping facilities and a beach.

Turn right onto 190th Street at 8 miles. Here's where things start getting a little strange; you'll have no choice but to turn left, then right, then left again—and the road names change with each turn. Don't worry about it; just follow the road to a left turn onto 196th/West Lake Shore Drive at 10 miles. This will take you near the lake shore, past lakefront homes, to a stop at County K, 11 miles. Turn right here, cross the bridge, and follow County K as it swings back to the right. At 11.9 miles K will go left; go straight here onto 70th Avenue/Forest Drive.

The next 5 miles seem confusing on paper, with the numbered street names changing almost as the road bends, but it's actually easy to ride: Turn right onto Moon Lake Drive/74th Avenue at 12.2 miles. Disregard the confusing numbers and stay on Moon Lake Drive to a right on Pine Harbor Drive at 13.7 miles. Again ignoring the numbered street names, stay on Pine Harbor Drive to a right turn onto Bay Road/75th Avenue at 15.2 miles. Turn left onto Lake Wissota Drive at a "T" intersection at 16 miles, then right onto Pine Harbor District Road/190th Street at 17.5 miles. This will snake you through a quiet, wooded, scenic residential peninsula that juts into the southern side of the lake. The road twists and turns, with a few small hills and some nice views of the lake off to the right. No matter what road you're on, if the lake is to the right, you'll do fine.

Pine Harbor District Road brings you to a right turn onto County X at 18.2 miles, a newly resurfaced, flat, straight road. Starting at 19.4 miles, a bridge crosses a portion of the lake. There's a wayside before the bridge and places to stop for food or drink all along here. Turn right onto County J at 20.3 miles. It's narrow, but there's not a lot of traffic. After a slight hill there's a fine run, mostly downhill, for much of the next 3 miles. Pass the grounds of the Northern Wisconsin Center for the Developmentally Disabled at 22.6 miles and the plant for Chippewa Springs Mineral Water at 23.2 miles; then turn right onto Highway 29/124.

This will bring you up and over a bridge that crosses the Chippewa River. Get up on the sidewalk to avoid the traffic and stay on the sidewalk as the road comes down and into Chippewa Falls. There's a nice view of the buildings of the city and the river below.

At the bottom of the bridge, 24 miles, turn right onto River Street East (Highway 124/178). From here it's easiest to simply follow the Highway 124 signs through town. After the right on River Street, Highway 124 turns left one block later onto Rushman Street, with the city center to the left. Follow the 124 signs straight as Highway 178 goes to the right at 24.3 miles. Highway 124 will become High Street, then Jefferson Street. Pass Leinenkugel's Brewery at 24.8 miles on the right and come back to the park entrance at 25 miles on the left.

# St. Croix Freefall

| | |
|---:|:---|
| **Number of miles:** | 23.9 (28.9 with park roads included) |
| **Approximate pedaling time:** | 3 hours |
| **Terrain:** | Hilly throughout; some flat and rolling stretches |
| **Traffic:** | Light |
| **Things to see:** | Interstate Park, several lakes, grand vistas, St. Croix Falls |
| **Food:** | St. Croix Falls; Dressler at 6.4 miles; Nyes at 12.9 miles |

This is one spectacular ride that will have you wondering why Wisconsin is called "America's Dairyland"—the "Midwest Mountain State" might be more appropriate. Geologists believe that millions of years ago there were mountains here that were taller than the Rockies. What remains are ridges of those mountains, with significant enough elevation change to provide spectacular views and plenty of challenges for all bicyclists.

Recognizing the need to protect and preserve a unique section of the St. Croix Riverway, Wisconsin and Minnesota became the first states in the nation to establish an "interstate" park, with separate "Interstate Parks" on each side of the St. Croix River. Wisconsin's Interstate Park, the start of this ride, became the first of its many state parks. It took Mother Nature millions of years to create the deep, 200-foot gorge known as the Dalles of the St. Croix River. As recently—in geological time, anyway—as 10,000 years ago, the finishing touches of what we see today were being applied when the last glacier rolled across the area, although the forces of nature continue to chip away at the steep walls of the Dalles.

Take some time to explore the park, where roads cut through the dense forest and lead to a secluded lake and the banks of the river. Wildlife, particularly deer, are abundant in the park as well as along the route of the ride; keep your eyes open for the white tails. The park alone is worthy of its own bike ride, with more than 5 miles of paved roads and 200 feet of elevation gain and loss through spectacular and rugged scenery within its boundaries.

The ride begins at the parking lot of the park headquarters. Turn right on Highway 35 and ride its paved shoulder 1.2 miles to a right turn onto County S. The fun begins immediately with a nearly 1-mile-long downhill run along the outer boundary of the park. The view is stunning: the rolling hills of Minnesota across the river, the park on the right, and woods and fields on the left. Control your descent, however, as you'll twist and turn down the road to a marshland at 1.9 miles and finally bottom out at 2.1 miles. You'll wind around some more, climb slightly, then pass 113th Avenue at 2.8 miles, where a look back up the ridge lets you know the kind of cycling ahead of you.

For some reason I've yet been able to figure out, western Wisconsin has a penchant for giving its back roads high street numbers—113th Avenue? Eventually, the ride crosses 210th Avenue. (None of the roads, by the way, are true "avenues" at all.) I think whoever was in charge of naming streets either had a pretty good sense of humor or none at all.

Just past 113th Avenue, at 3.3 miles, the road squeezes between some enormous boulders at the edges of the road before opening up somewhat at 3.7 miles; the river can be seen through the trees to the left. Look at the high ridge to your left—at 3.9 miles you'll turn left onto 100th Avenue and begin your climb to the top of that ridge.

This portion of the ride starts with a drop through valley farmland; then the climb begins. Despite the look of the ridge, the climb lasts for only a mile. It provides a little respite at 4.5 miles, where you get a slight downhill into a tight S turn before cresting the ridge at 5 miles. From here it's a reasonably flat run

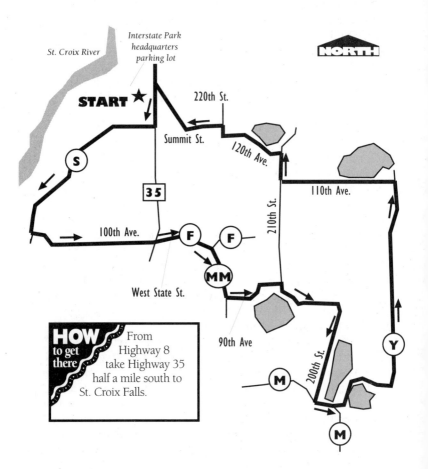

**DIREC-TIONS at a glance**

| | |
|---|---|
| 0.0 | Begin at the Interstate Park headquarters parking lot. |
| 0.2 | Turn right onto Highway 35. |
| 1.2 | Turn right onto County S. |
| 3.9 | Turn left onto 100th Avenue. |
| 6.4 | Cross Highway 35 to West State Street/County F. |
| 7.5 | Turn right onto County MM. |
| 8.4 | Turn left onto 90th Avenue. |
| 9.7 | Continue right on 90th past 210th Street. |
| 10.8 | Turn right onto 200th Street. |
| 12.7 | Turn left onto County M. |
| 12.9 | Turn left onto County Y. |
| 16.8 | Continue past County F on County Y. |
| 17.8 | Turn left onto 110th Avenue. |
| 18.3 | Continue past 195th Avenue. |
| 19.3 | Turn right onto 210th Avenue. |
| 20.3 | Turn left onto 120th Avenue. |
| 21.3 | Turn right onto 220th Street. |
| 21.5 | Turn left onto Summit Street. |
| 23.5 | Turn left onto Highway 35. |
| 23.7 | Turn right into park entrance. |
| 23.9 | Return to parking lot. |

into the small town of Dressler at 6.4 miles, where you can take a break for food or beverages. The mile climb is well worth the initial spectacular run down and along the bottom of the valley.

Cross Highway 35 on West State Street, which blends into County F. The road climbs a bit and swings around the ridge to the junction with County MM; follow MM to the right at 7.5 miles. It probably won't surprise you at all to see the Trollhaugen Alpine Ski Center on your right, with the chairlifts rising to the top of the ridge. After passing a racetrack on the right, turn left at 8.4 miles onto 90th Avenue.

A downhill starts you on the way to Lotus Lake and Lotus Lake Park. After curving north around the top of the lake at 8.8 miles and passing the park, with a picnic area and campground, you'll stop at the intersection with 210th Avenue at 9.7 miles; turn right and continue down 90th. Passing through a swampy marshland north of the lake, the road climbs some more to a vista of distant ridges capped by barns and silos. A quick drop at 10.6 miles brings a stop sign and a right turn onto 200th Avenue and into a picturesque valley.

The next couple of miles feature some pleasant downhill runs and views of Horse Lake on the left. At 12.3 miles the road pulls away from the lake, crosses a set of abandoned railroad tracks, and intersects with County M at 12.7 miles. A right heads into Nyes for refreshments. Turn left and follow M to County Y at 12.9 miles; head left on Y up and around the other side of Horse Lake. County Y follows tight to the shore of the lake to 13.9 miles, then breaks east over the top of Round Lake before turning north for a pleasant, straight ride of reasonably gentle ups and downs through farm country. Pass County F at 16.8 miles and then turn left onto 110th Avenue at 17.8 miles.

Sand Lake is to the north, and you'll pass a church on the banks of the lake at 18.3 miles. Continuing straight through farmland and fields, passing 195th Street on the left and crossing 200th Street at 18.8 miles, stop at 210th Street and turn right. A half mile ahead turn left at Poplar Lake onto 120th Avenue and follow along the lake, passing Ravine Street to the left. The lake is in view all along this stretch. At 21.3 miles the road swings 90 degrees to the right onto 220th Street to a left onto Summit Street at 21.5 miles.

This is the home stretch and pretty much downhill all the way. Watch out for the rough railroad tracks at 22.3 miles and a couple of sharp turns. At 23.5 you're back at Highway 35. Turn left, and the park entrance is just ahead on the right. To get into the city of St. Croix without riding on busy Highway 35, cross the highway here and follow the road into the city.

### Gandy Dancer Trail

A trailhead for the 50-mile Gandy Dancer Trail is in St. Croix. Go to the Polk County Information Center, a half mile north on Highway 35 from Interstate Park's entrance, for current access information.

# Blue Hills Ascent

| | |
|---|---|
| **Number of miles:** | 28.8 |
| **Approximate pedaling time:** | 3 hours |
| **Terrain:** | Gradual climbs, some steep; flat stretches and rolling hills |
| **Traffic:** | Moderate on Highways 8 and 40; light elsewhere |
| **Things to see:** | Incredible sweeping panoramic views of an ancient mountain range |
| **Food:** | Bruce; Weyerhauser at 18.6 miles |

Traveling along Highway 8 can be deceiving. The highway appears virtually flat, surrounded by a swampy lowland in many areas, with little variation in elevation as it cuts across the central area of northern Wisconsin, yet just to the north and south of the highway are some impressive hills that offer incredible views of the surrounding countryside. Nowhere is this more evident than in the Blue Hills north and west of Bruce. Even this bike ride is deceiving. Granted, you gain a fair amount of elevation, but the grades are not as gruelingly steep as in the Driftless area of southwestern Wisconsin. You will climb on this ride, but it's broken by long, relatively flat stretches, some wonderful downhills, and some rolling terrain.

Begin at the intersection of Highways 8 and 40 in Bruce, a small town that proudly proclaims itself the "Gateway to the Blue Hills." You might ask, "What hills? I don't see any hills." Trust me—you'll see them soon enough.

Follow Highway 40 north as it turns left just past the downtown area, then north and out of town. At County O, 1.1 miles, turn left. Now you'll see the hills, those ridges off straight and to

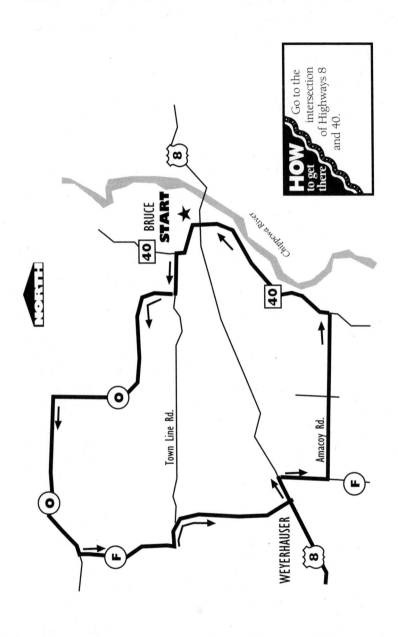

**DIREC-TIONS at a glance**

| | |
|---|---|
| 0.0 | Begin in Bruce, at intersection of Highways 8 and 40. |
| 0.1 | Go north on Highway 40 and curve to the left through town. |
| 0.8 | Curve to the right and north through town. |
| 1.1 | Turn left onto County O. |
| 2.1 | Follow County O right. |
| 2.9 | Follow County O left. |
| 5.3 | Follow County O right. |
| 7.5 | Follow County O left. |
| 11.9 | Turn left onto County F. |
| 18.6 | Turn left onto Highway 8. |
| 19.2 | Turn right onto County F. |
| 20.7 | Turn left onto Amacoy Road. |
| 22.7 | Cross Hutchinson Road. |
| 24.6 | Turn left onto Highway 40. |
| 28.8 | Return to Bruce, at intersection of Highways 8 and 40. |

the right. At one time thought to be part of the oldest mountain range in the country, and more impressive than the Rockies according to some geologists, Mother Nature has spent millions of years whittling them down to their present form.

Getting to the Blue Hills is a simple matter of following County O as it goes right, left, then right again. Head east first for a flat mile through corn fields, then north, and across a creek at 2.4 miles; then follow County O left at 2.8 miles. There is a gentle grade here that will continue through fields and, now, a few trees. The grade gets gradually steeper and tops off at 3.4 miles. Take a look around; it might not seem like it, but the elevation—and the view of the remote countryside in all directions—tells you that you're in the foothills of the Blue Hills.

A downhill at 3.9 miles bottoms out at a creek crossing at 4.4 miles, followed immediately by a climb, steep at the beginning then lessening, to 5 miles. Just ahead County O turns to the north with another climb, followed by a downhill run heading to the hills, which are quite clearly in the distance. At 6.2 miles it levels a bit, then drops. Look ahead to the road that climbs straight up the wooded hillside and take comfort in the fact that you'll turn left and not have to climb that one. At 6.9 miles there's another creek crossing, some downhill, and a rise; then the road takes a left at 7.2 miles.

The farm fields have been left behind now, and a dense forest provides the scenery. Up in the hills there are fewer grand vistas than there were during the climb. Cross another creek at 7 miles. Pass the entrance to the Blue Hills Cross Country Ski Trails at 7.2 miles and, a little farther on, pass the entrance to Christie Mountain Alpine Ski Center. The climb continues, occasionally offering a dip, until 8.8 miles.

After climbing for the better part of 7 miles, it's time to enjoy the fruits of your labor. For the next 2 miles, you'll pretty much be coasting downhill, bending first left, then right, through a thick forest that offers just the occasional glimpse of land below. At 10.8 miles you'll bottom out briefly into a swampy area, stop at the intersection with County F, and then turn left onto F.

The road heads downhill for almost 5 miles, winding through S turns, past small pothole lakes, and picturesque wetlands. At 15.2 miles the countryside below fills the horizon. By 16.4 miles you're back into farmland and heading into the tiny town of Weyerhauser, passing the ballpark at 17.9 miles, going through the main street, and making a stop at Highway 8 at 18.6 miles. Fill your water bottles, have a bite to eat, and get ready for the last 10 miles.

The Blue Hills are behind you, but there still is fun and scenic riding ahead. Turn left onto Highway 8 and ride the paved shoulder to a right onto County F at 19.2 miles. After a climb up from the highway, enjoy a nice downhill into farm country to a left onto Amacoy Road at 20.7 miles.

Amacoy is a remarkable 7-mile-long roller coaster of a ride, with some wonderful vistas in all directions; farm fields leave the views wide open. If you encounter any traffic at all, it will likely be farm vehicles, the mailman, or local residents heading into or home from town. Cross Hutchinson Road at 22.7 miles, endure a brief but gradual climb, and then sit back for a pleasant downhill marred only by a junkyard at 23.5 miles. You'll soon cross a creek, climb a bit, and then find a relatively flat road to a stop sign at 27.5 miles. Turn left onto Highway 40.

There is no paved shoulder on the 4.2-mile ride on Highway 40 back to Bruce, but the traffic is remarkably light for a state highway. There is a gravel shoulder if you are uncomfortable riding the highway when traffic passes. The highway winds somewhat with a few ups and downs (no long or steep hills) and comes back to Highway 8 at 28.8 miles.

# Webster Tour of Lakes

| | |
|---:|:---|
| **Number of miles:** | 21.9 |
| **Approximate pedaling time:** | 2.5 hours |
| **Terrain:** | Flat to varied, with some rolling hills |
| **Traffic:** | Moderate on Highway 35; light elsewhere |
| **Things to see:** | Gandy Dancer Trail, numerous lakes |
| **Food:** | Stores and restaurants at the start and at 11.4 miles |

Northern Wisconsin's Vilas County has a well-earned reputation as a vacation destination because of its hundreds of pristine inland lakes. Not many people know that Polk, Barron, Washburn, and Burnett Counties in the northeastern wedge of the state can match Vilas lake for lake. Pale blue dots cover the map north and east of Webster in the middle of Burnett County, where this ride takes place, and you'll get a good look at six of these lakes.

The ride begins where it will end, at County U in downtown Webster, where you'll find plenty of restaurants, places to stay, and small-town, tourist-oriented craft and gift shops. Ride north on Highway 35 to a right turn onto County A at 1.2 miles. A paved shoulder makes the moderate highway traffic bearable. County A starts with a slight uphill S turn and then quickly flattens out as Devil's Lake comes into view to the left. Much of this ride will feature the twisting nature of roads around lakes, following the natural flow of the terrain. At 3.2 miles the road begins to leave the lake behind and leads into farmers' fields on the way to County T at 5.2 miles.

Turn left onto County T and head north on a half-moon

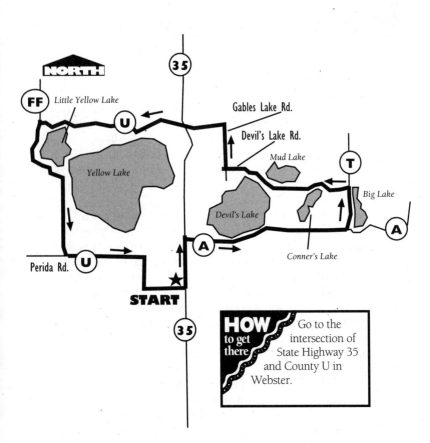

NORTH

35

FF  *Little Yellow Lake*

Gables Lake Rd.

U

Devil's Lake Rd.

*Mud Lake*

T

*Yellow Lake*

*Big Lake*

*Devil's Lake*

A

*Conner's Lake*

Perida Rd.  U

A

START

35

**HOW**
to get
there

Go to the intersection of State Highway 35 and County U in Webster.

**DIREC-TIONS at a glance**

0.0 Head north from County U on Highway 35.
1.2 Turn right onto County A.
5.2 Turn left onto County T.
6.2 Turn left onto Devil's Lake Road.
9.5 Turn right onto Gables Lake Road.
10.4 Turn left onto County U.
11.4 Cross Highway 35.
14.9 Continue left on County U past County FF.
18.4 Continue left past Perida Road.
21.9 Return to County U at Highway 35.

curve past a lowland, marshy corner of Big Lake on the left. You'll climb up and out onto some gently rolling terrain before once again seeing the lake at 5.9 miles. Just ahead—and keep your eyes open because it's easy to miss—at 6.2 miles, is a left turn onto Devil's Lake Road. You'll be hard-pressed to find more beautiful lake riding anywhere as you roll west on Devil's Lake Road, with its overhanging tree branches, gentle curves, and slightly rolling terrain (Conner's Lake is to your left). Pass John Lake Road at 7.3 miles and enter some fields, then forests. John Lake is off to the right. A thick cover of trees edges the road, and a few cottages line the lake shore. A short downhill brings you to a beautiful spot at 8.2 miles between John Lake on the right and Devil's Lake on the left. With a parking area, boat landing, and beach, it's a perfect spot to stop for a rest and a cool swim.

Devil's Lake Road continues north, curving and winding its way over the top of Devil's Lake to the intersection with Gables Lake Road at 9.5 miles. Turn right on Gables for a mile through farmers' fields and past Bushey Road to the intersection with County U at 10.4 miles. Turn left onto County U and immediately ride a roller coaster up and down, passing a pine plantation and a few homes on the way to Highway 35 at 11.4 miles.

The ride continues on an official Wisconsin "Rustic Road," so designated for its charm and beauty. There are still two lakes to wind past before returning to Webster, and the first comes quickly. Just past the highway the road crosses the Gandy Dancer Trail, a converted rail-trail with a packed-limestone surface. You could hop on the trail here and, in 5.8 miles, be back at Webster.

Staying on County U, you'll pass a supper club at 11.8 miles, a golf course at 12.2 miles, and a fairly flat, straight section of road north of Yellow Lake. A downhill at 14.3 miles crosses a bridge where the Yellow River flows into Little Yellow Lake. The nicest section of the second half of the ride begins here.

The lake stays in sight to the left as the narrow, forested road winds, curves, dips, and rises its way around. There's little traffic to spoil the ride. At 14.9 miles County FF blends into County U from the north; stay to the left and continue around the lake on County U. At 17.2 miles County U comes back briefly to Yellow Lake, bends to the south, and flattens out through open fields before coming into a slightly more forested area just before Perida Road.

Continue to the left past Perida Road at 18.4 miles for a nearly straight shot on County U—you'll have to negotiate two flat 90-degree turns—right back into Webster. Approaching the city limits, County U adopts the name Hickory Street. Just before coming to Highway 35 and the end of the ride at 21.9 miles, you'll again cross over the Gandy Dancer Trail. If you have the time, ride up the trail to County U and swing around the lakes again; it's worth it.

# Hayward Lakes:
# Where Eagles Soar

| | |
|---:|:---|
| Number of miles: | 27.1 |
| Approximate pedaling time: | 3 hours |
| Terrain: | Flat to gently rolling |
| Traffic: | Light |
| Things to see: | Secluded lakes, wildlife, small resort communities |
| Food: | At the start; resort/restaurants at 9 miles; store at 11.9 miles; resort at 16.2 miles; restaurants, taverns, and resorts from 22.6 miles |

It was chance, really; just dumb luck. I stopped at about 17 miles, where the road hopscotches across a couple of small islands on Lake Chippewa, to take in the view. Out of the corner of my eye, I caught a glimpse of something flashing by and I turned to see a bald eagle swooping across the water not 50 yards away from me. As I watched the eagle ride thermals higher and higher right above me, another eagle swooped across the water and circled up to join the other. After ten minutes or so they tired of the game and glided away. Leaving the eagles, I rode a few hundred yards up the road and flushed a blue heron that had been hidden in some tall grasses next to the road, at the water's edge. That's just the way it is in the deep Northwoods of Wisconsin.

This wonderful ride provides a real taste of backwoods northern Wisconsin lake country as it circles the waters of Lake Chippewa, a large lake with numerous bays and islands, which

was formed by a dam on the Chippewa River. This is the Northwoods of small rustic cottages and fishing resorts, of bears, loons, and eagles. This is the Northwoods of the Lac Courte Oreilles Indian Reservation, a special place to the people whose ancestors were here long before the first European settlers came to the continent.

Park at the small resort community between Big Round Lake and Little Round Lake on County B. It's not a town, really, just a collection of resorts, small restaurants, and stores. Go west on B a half mile to a left turn onto County NN. Soon the houses will be left behind, and you'll be riding a fairly flat road—gently rolling at best—through a heavily forested area of pines, aspens, and poplars. Just past Squaw Bay Road at 5.2 miles, the forest thins a bit, and at 6.5 miles you'll cross a small portion of the bay and continue past a cranberry bog on the left. The road picks up a bit more roll here, passing a barren clear-cut, although trees do line the road.

Turn left at 8.8 miles onto County N/CC. At 9 miles County CC turns sharply to the right, but it also goes straight; follow it straight ahead. Just past Conger's Road at 9.5 miles (there are a couple of restaurant choices here if you want to take a break), you'll see Chief Lake to the left. The road is fairly straight here, with some gentle climbing as you pass the Lac Courte Oreilles Fish Hatchery at 11 miles and ride through a wetland a half mile later. A gas station/general store (open seven days a week) is at 11.9 miles. Go past Blueberry Lake on the right at 12.3 miles, a small bridge over a Lake Chippewa backwater at 12.7 miles, and then straight past the turn onto County H at 12.8 miles. Milwaukee Bay can be seen through the trees to the left at 13.6 miles; you'll continue to catch glimpses of it for the next mile.

County CC veers to the right at 15 miles in the little Lac Courte Oreilles village of New Post. The road winds and twists to the Big Musky Resort (open 365 days a year) at 16.2 miles, then to a jump between small islands across Lake Chippewa at 17.2 miles, the spot where I watched the eagles soar. Crossing to an island at 18.1 miles, the road weaves, with the lake to the

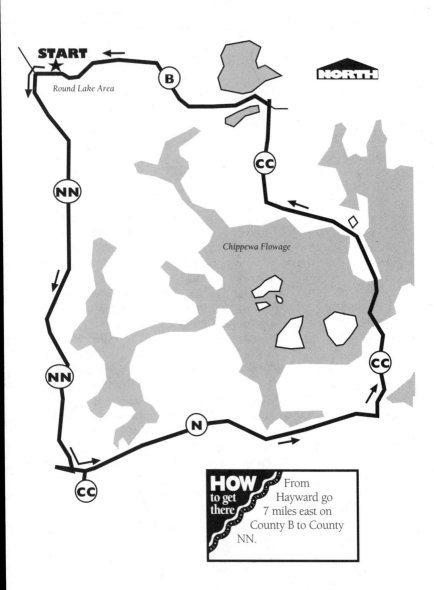

START

Round Lake Area

B

NORTH

NN

Chippewa Flowage

CC

CC

NN

N

CC

**HOW** to get there — From Hayward go 7 miles east on County B to County NN.

**DIREC-TIONS at a glance**

0.0 At Round Lake Area, go west on County B.
0.5 Turn left onto County NN.
8.8 Turn left onto County N/County CC.
9.0 Continue on County CC.
22.6 Turn left onto County B.
27.1 Return to Round Lake area.

south and Kavanagh Bay to the north.

Stop and admire the towering old-growth pines at 19.3 miles—there aren't many trees like this left in the United States. The road veers left and right, S turning through here, gently rolling through the forest. At 21.7 miles pass the intersection with Kelly Road/Twin Bay Road; then move on to a left turn onto County B at 22.6 miles.

Restaurants, a motel, bait store, groceries, and a cafe can refresh you before the last few miles along County B, which offers the most varied terrain of the ride. Reed Lake is to the left, before a couple of pretty good hills at 24.8 miles. A number of restaurants will entice you along this rolling rustic road, not the least of which might be Dave's Barbecue Shack at 26.5 miles. Just ahead, at 27.2 miles, is the small resort community—it's not even a town, just a collection of businesses that cater to the tourist trade—where you started.

# Waterfall Wander

| | |
|---:|:---|
| Number of miles: | 14.4 |
| Approximate pedaling time: | 1.5 hours |
| Terrain: | Flat to rolling, with one steep hill |
| Traffic: | Moderate on Highway 35; light elsewhere |
| Things to see: | Grand vistas, Gandy Dancer Trail, Pattison State Park, Big Manitou Falls |
| Food: | Small stores at 8.2 miles; bar/restaurant at 8.3 miles; bar/restaurant at 10.5 miles |

This ride begins or ends (or both) with a short hike. From the main Pattison State Park parking lot on Highway 35, go a quarter mile south on Highway 35 to a right turn onto County B. There's a small parking lot immediately to the left (you could also park here to start the ride). Walk across the road to the trail that leads back to Big Manitou Falls on the Black River. Stay on the trail to the right for no more than 100 yards; you'll hear the rush of Wisconsin's highest waterfall before you even get close. At Big Manitou Falls the Black River cascades 165 feet over the Superior Escarpment, an impressive site for beginning or ending a bike ride. Follow the trail west for another look at this impressive natural wonder from several different viewing platforms. The Superior Escarpment, a ridge that cuts through this portion of Douglas County, provides the platform for some spectacular bike riding. Once at the heart of the Copper Rush of the late 1800s, much of the area today is still remote and rugged country.

After leaving the falls, ride slowly west on County B, enjoy-

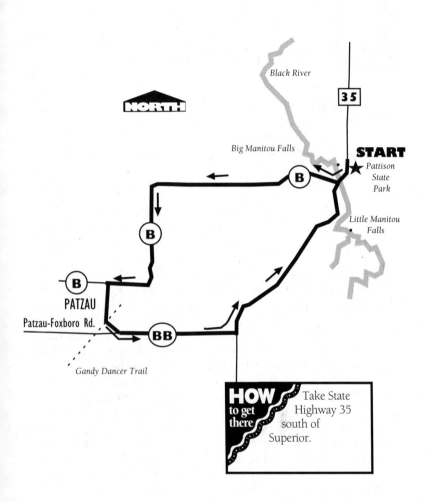

**DIREC-TIONS at a glance**

| | |
|---|---|
| 0.0 | From the entrance to Pattison State Park, go south on Highway 35. |
| 0.2 | Turn right onto County B. |
| 6.9 | Turn left onto County BB. |
| 7.3 | Continue past intersection with Patzau-Foxboro Road. |
| 7.5 | Continue east on County BB. |
| 10.4 | Turn left onto Highway 35. |
| 14.4 | Return to entrance to Pattison Park. |

ing the impressive view: Superior-Duluth and Lake Superior are off to your right, and the hills of Minnesota are off in the distance in front of you. The terrain is gently rolling as you pass an abandoned tavern at 1.2 miles and a church at 1.4 miles.

Continuing west, the countryside changes to less forest and more hardscrabble farmland, flat and marshy. Passing a horse farm at 1.9 miles, the scenery opens up with some gentle roller-coaster hills starting around 3.6 miles. County B swings south at 4.1 miles and stays smooth, flat, and straight past homes and farms. A bit of a dip and an S turn takes you south and west again through a forest of small poplars, birches, and aspens.

Turn left onto County BB at 6.9 miles (if you miss the turn, in 3 miles you'll end up in Minnesota). The forest begins closing in at 7.3 miles before the small town of Patzau and the north portion of the Gandy Dancer Trail, not to be confused with the more developed southern portion of the trail in Polk and Burnett Counties. Here the trail is a bit rough for bicycling; it is more suitable for horseback riding or snowmobiling in winter. There's a small store and gas station a quarter mile down Patzau-Foxboro Road from County BB and the Trail's End Bar and Restaurant on County BB at 8.2 miles.

County BB takes a 90-degree swing to the east just after the

Gandy Dancer Trail, and it's time to earn the nice ride down off the Superior Escarpment. A hill starting at 8.3 miles levels off a bit at 8.5 miles, then begins a steady grind to 9.1 miles. Take a break here and look off behind you at the hills of Minnesota. The forest is in much tighter here, with a few homes set back in the trees. The terrain takes on a series of small roller-coaster rides before a dip at 9.9 miles. In a half mile you're back at Highway 35. Although a state highway, traffic is light by comparison with highways in more populated areas. The intersection provides two opportunities for food and drink before the final 4 miles back to Pattison. A paved shoulder and good visibility make for a safe ride as Highway 35 negotiates a few sweeping curves and moderate ups and downs before the intersection with County B and the park entrance.

Before leaving take a walk or a ride through Pattison State Park. A self-guided walk shows where, long ago, copper miners looked for ore. An interpretive center details the fish, birds, and mammals of the area as well as the geology and history. The park also has a lake—famous in the logging-era days as a holding pond to keep logs from crashing over the falls—with a public swimming beach. Little Manitou Falls, about a mile's walk upstream, carries the Black River into the lake. More waterfalls can be found 17 miles away on the Amicon River at Amicon River State Park.

# Bayfield Orchard Blast

| | |
|---:|:---|
| Number of miles: | 10.6 |
| Approximate pedaling time: | 1.5 hours |
| Terrain: | Very hilly |
| Traffic: | Moderate on Highway 13; light on County J |
| Things to see: | General tourist attractions of Bayfield, fruit orchards in the countryside, outstanding vistas of ridges, Lake Superior, and Apostle Islands |
| Food: | Numerous restaurants in Bayfield; fruit and drink at any of seven orchards along the ride |

The Bayfield Peninsula, which juts out into Lake Superior, is one of Wisconsin's more beautiful spots. Rugged, hilly, and untamed throughout much of the interior of the peninsula, the small towns of Washburn and Bayfield offer unexpected creature comforts that range from elegant dining to stately Victorian mansions converted to bed and breakfast inns. The waters of Lake Superior and the chain of twenty-two Apostle Islands, just off the peninsula, provide spectacular boating and opportunities for exploration.

Although Bayfield is Wisconsin's second-largest county, the locals boast that there isn't a single stop light to be found—good news for bicyclists. On the downside, bicycling possibilities are somewhat limited because of an unusual (for Wisconsin, anyway) lack of paved roads and the extremely hilly terrain up from the shore into the interior of the peninsula. For the cyclist willing to take on the hills, however, the rewards are many, not the

least of which is some spectacular scenery reminiscent of more mountainous states. Besides the scenery this ride is a fruit-picker's delight, as it winds its way past raspberry, blueberry, and apple orchards.

The ride begins at the Washington Avenue parking lot for the ferry that connects Bayfield to nearby Madeline Island in the Chequamegon Bay. Head west one or two blocks, depending where you parked, to a left on First Street (Highway 13). The highway winds through town, so you'll have plenty of opportunities to stop for an ice cream, a cappuccino, or a bite to eat before heading up into the hills. Go one block south on First Street; then turn right on Rittenhouse Avenue (there isn't a sign at the intersection, but just be sure to stay on Highway 13 through town). The first taste of climbing begins right away as you head up Rittenhouse for six blocks, about a half mile from the start, to a left turn on Sixth Street. Ahead you can see Chequamegon Bay and Madeline Island. Highway 13 (Sixth Street) bears right at seven-tenths of a mile, then begins a gradual uphill. The posted speed limit here is 35 mph and increases to 55 mph, but a paved shoulder keeps you out of the traffic.

Turn right onto Highway J, at 1.5 miles, and get ready to climb for the next mile. Halfway up you'll crest the first hill, then level out a bit before the grade picks up again to 2.4 miles. Take a break at the top and look out at the ridges off in the distance; the clean runs from an alpine ski area are on a far ridge, and the blue waters of the bay are behind and to the southeast. Near the road in the valley below is the first of many orchards offering fresh raspberries and blueberries in early summer.

Go downhill to 2.9 miles, turn right at the stop sign, and continue on County J. More forested ridges lay over a valley to your left as you begin another climb, which, at 3.1 miles, flattens out about as much as it ever does in this area. The scenery through the ride is stunning, with farms tucked in the valleys and a few private residences tucked in the hillside ridges that rise on all sides.

County J turns right at 3.8 miles and continues to curve

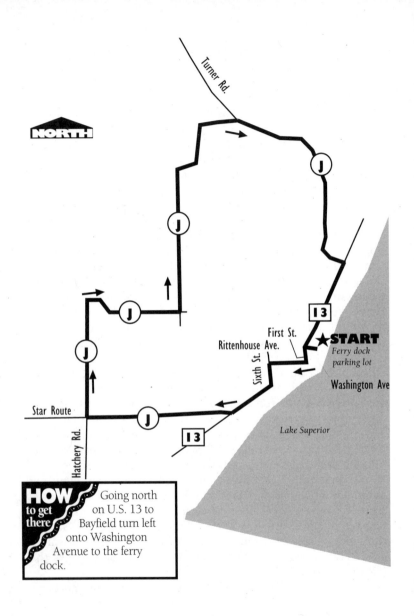

NORTH

Turner Rd.

J

J

J

J

J

J

Star Route

Hatchery Rd.

13

13

First St.

Rittenhouse Ave.

Sixth St.

★ **START**

*Ferry dock
parking lot*

**Washington Ave**

*Lake Superior*

**HOW**
to get
there
Going north
on U.S. 13 to
Bayfield turn left
onto Washington
Avenue to the ferry
dock.

**DIREC-TIONS at a glance**

0.0 From ferry-dock parking lot, turn left onto First Street (Highway 13).

0.1 After one block, turn right onto Rittenhouse Avenue (Highway 13).

0.5 Turn left onto Sixth Street (Highway 13).

1.5 Turn right onto County J.

2.9 At the stop sign turn right, continuing on County J.

3.9 Turn right again on County J.

5.0 Turn left on County J and follow road around.

9.7 Turn right onto Highway 13.

10.6 Turn left onto Washington Avenue and return to ferry dock.

right, climbing all the while, easing a bit at 4.2 miles, then pitching steeply upward again to the crest a 4.7 miles. At 5 miles County J turns right at the stop sign. If you've had enough of the hills, continue straight on County I and back into Bayfield. If you stick with the ride, however, keep in mind that there are only 2.5 miles more of the rolling stuff and then you get a wonderful downhill nearly all the way back to Bayfield.

Turn left on County J and climb, again, past a winery and more berry farms and apple orchards for another mile. Things begin to level out a bit before the road bears to the right at 6.4 miles, then left and back to the right at 7 miles. Look off to the right at the hills you've climbed through and pat yourself on the back. Now the real fun begins.

With the hills behind you and Lake Superior off in the distance, you begin the freefall. Turner Road intersects at 7.4 miles—traffic from Turner Road stops; you don't. Stay on Highway J to the right. You'll zig and zag as the road winds down and levels out a bit 7.6 miles, only to find another good downhill at 8 miles as you dip through a forest. The road continues like this, weaving left and right to a steeper descent at 9.3 miles and a fairly sharp bend to the left at 9.5 miles, where you'll again see the bay as you approach Highway 13.

A paved shoulder carries you into town, with one last good descent at 10.2 miles. Enjoy the view of the bay and Madeline Island off in the distance. At 10.6 miles you're back at Washington Avenue and the ferry dock.

# Riding with the Apostles

| | |
|---|---|
| **Number of miles:** | 8.9 (12.9 with side trip to either state or town parks; add 2 more miles with cemetery side trip) |
| **Approximate pedaling time:** | 1 hour |
| **Terrain:** | Flat, with gradual hills |
| **Traffic:** | Light |
| **Things to see:** | Museum, Indian Burial Ground, Lake Superior shoreline, Big Bay State Park, Big Bay Town Park |
| **Food:** | Numerous restaurants in La Pointe; restaurant at 1.2 miles |

Madeline Island is the most accessible—and commercialized—of the Apostle Islands archipelago at the tip of Bayfield Peninsula in Lake Superior. Although the vast majority of these small islands are uninhabited, protected, and can be reached only by watercraft, regular ferry service connects Madeline to the mainland. A historic Ojibway homeland for hundreds of years prior to European exploration, the island later became an important fur-trading outpost for the French, British, and Americans; its history is honored at a local museum. At present the island is primarily a tourist destination and an escape for the well-to-do, with stately homes tucked in the forests along the water's edge. A state park and town park provide excellent camping facilities and access to Lake Superior.

The tour begins at the ferry dock—ferries run more than hourly throughout the summer months—in La Pointe, the only town on the island. La Pointe is filled with gift shops, restau-

rants, taverns, small inns, and lodging, the latter ranging from rustic to elegant. From the ferry landing turn left onto Main Street (the museum is directly across the street); then take the next right onto Big Bay Road (also County Highway H). A gradual uphill takes you through the edge of town. You'll pass an old schoolhouse on the right, an old cemetery, an old church on the right, and a scattering of historic buildings that date back more than one hundred years. The town is small—there are only a few hundred year-round residents—and you'll quickly head out on a forested roadway. Mixed hardwoods, pines, and cedars tower along the road's edge, and a soft carpet of ferns seems to glow beneath the trees. Less than a mile into the ride the road begins to level off. Gravel driveways, many gated or otherwise blocked, cut into the trees to the left, protecting the stately homes along the shoreline from unwanted visitors.

The last chance for food is at 1.2 miles on the left, a small restaurant/tavern, until the ride ends back in La Pointe. Another gradual ascent through the forest begins here and continues for the next mile. At 1.6 miles the island's airport appears on the right, carved out of a thick forest that now obscures a view of Lake Superior. At 2.2 miles, where the road levels and begins a gradual descent, the lake can again be glimpsed through the trees, as well as a few of the homes tucked along the lakeshore.

The roadways are somewhat narrow through the island, but traffic is light and respectful of cyclists. Just ahead, at 2.9 miles, the road bends to the right, but not before providing an unobstructed view of Chequamegon Bay, Basswood Island, and the mainland. A gradual uphill continues past a sharp bend to the left at 3.3 miles and a right at 3.5 miles. Finally, at 3.8 miles, the road levels out again.

At 4 miles County H continues to the left and eventually turns into a gravel road. To get to Big Bay Town Park—with camping, showers, and a beach, although a swim in Lake Superior's cold waters is more chore than pleasure—continue for 2 miles on County H. For the tour turn right for 1 mile on Black Shanty Road, following the sign to Big Bay State Park. At the

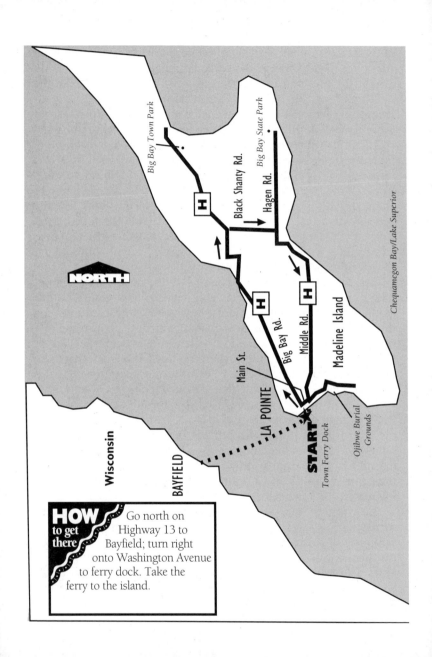

NORTH

Big Bay Town Park

Big Bay State Park

Black Shanty Rd.

Hagen Rd.

Chequamegon Bay/Lake Superior

H

Big Bay Rd.

Middle Rd.

Madeline Island

Main St.

LA POINTE

START

Town Ferry Dock

Ojibwe Burial Grounds

Wisconsin

BAYFIELD

**HOW** to get there Go north on Highway 13 to Bayfield; turn right onto Washington Avenue to ferry dock. Take the ferry to the island.

**DIREC-TIONS at a glance**

0.0  Turn left onto Main Street from ferry-dock parking lot.

0.1  Turn right onto Big Bay Road (also County H).

4.0  Turn right onto Black Shanty Road.

5.0  Turn right onto Middle Road.

5.8  Road bends right away from shoreline.

8.8  Turn right onto Main Street.

9.9  Return to ferry dock.

next intersection, Hagen Road, it's 2 miles to the left to Big Bay State Park. The state park features a campground, showers, picnic areas, a beach, and hiking trails.

To head back to La Pointe, turn right onto Middle Road, where Lake Superior soon appears in the distance. The road bends to the right at 5.8 miles for a mile-long ride along the rocky shoreline. Big Bay State Park is along the shoreline behind you; mainland Wisconsin and Michigan's Upper Peninsula are across the bay. The road here cuts between a few houses and a small beach with boat docks jutting out in the lake. At 6.8 miles the road swings back inland, down the middle of the island, and back to La Pointe.

Keep your eye out for deer along this stretch; the island's deer seem almost tame and often just cock their heads and watch you roll past, rather than leap into the woods. The forest isn't as thick here as it is on the road out from town; more homesteads appear as well as an occasional small farm. In less than a half mile, the payback for your previous climb begins as a gentle downhill takes you almost all the way back to town. In the distance the rise of hills on the mainland can be easily seen. More houses begin to appear at around 7.7 miles.

At 8.2 miles the road bears slightly to the right, crossing a small creek, and then swings back to the left and comes into the outskirts of La Pointe. The town softball field, pavilion, playground, tennis courts, and public washrooms are at 8.7 miles. On the right is Tom's Burned Down Cafe, certainly one of the more unusual businesses you'll likely encounter on any bike ride. Following a fire that destroyed a restaurant on the site, the owner brought in a railroad boxcar and reopened for business. Today the Burned Down Cafe is an open-air bar/restaurant that is a cobbled-together collection of structures, folk art, and, some would say, just plain junk. Main Street is just ahead at 8.8 miles, where a right turn for one block takes you back to the ferry dock.

A worthwhile, short side trip through town would be to visit the Ojibway Burial Ground. Turn left onto Main Street from Middle Road, passing the town park and beach on the right. At four-tenths of a mile, the road crosses a small creek, with the La Pointe Yacht Club on the right. Just ahead turn right onto Old Fort Road to Cemetery Road at eight-tenths of a mile. Follow Cemetery Road to the right; it dead ends in a parking lot for the Yacht Club at 1 mile. The cemetery is on the left. Established in 1836, the Christianized Ojibway adopted the European-style house as a grave cover to protect both the dead and food left for the dead. The small structures can be seen covering many of the graves. Follow the same route back to the ferry dock.

# Minocqua Lakes and Bearskin Trail Loop

| | |
|---|---|
| Number of miles: | 30.3 |
| Approximate pedaling time: | 3.5 hours |
| Terrain: | Slightly rolling |
| Traffic: | Light except on Highway 51 in Minocqua; moderate on County J leaving Minocqua |
| Things to see: | Minocqua, Northern Highlands State Forest, several lakes, the town of Lake Tomahawk, Bearskin Trail |
| Food: | In Minocqua; 15.4 miles at Lake Tomahawk; 23.3 miles at Highway 51; numerous resorts along the route |

Bears have a way of walking that, to me, is almost catlike. It's a fluid loping, head down, back arched, tentative yet assured. It's the sort of walk that says, "I'll leave you alone if you leave me alone." The first time I saw a bear in the wild was on a bike trip through northwestern Wisconsin. Riding along a densely forested road in the mid-afternoon of a hot, steamy August day, my companions and I looked ahead to see a catlike creature wander slowly across the road. Not sure at first what we were seeing, it hit us all at about the same time—bear! We were given the gift of seeing an elusive black bear in the wild. By the time we got to the spot where it crossed, it had already disappeared into the forest.

The only other time I saw a black bear in the wild was in late summer of 1996 as I was riding alone on the Bearskin Trail— while riding on *this* ride. The bear ambled slowly across the trail

about 75 yards in front of me, paused slightly, raising its head in my direction, and then continued its slow walk across the trail, concerned not the least by my presence. I coasted to a slow roll where the bear crossed the trail, and I peered into the thick forest, hoping for another glimpse, but it was gone.

Before you decide not to do this ride because I saw a bear on it, consider that Wisconsin's northern forests are thick with bear—you just don't see them often because they don't want to be seen. Bears want nothing to do with us and will almost always avoid our presence. Except in popular campgrounds in bear country, where food is a mere Coleman cooler away, bears steer clear of humans. Catching a glimpse of a bear in the wild is a rare treat, as the bear will be doing its best to avoid being seen and get as far from you as it can. I hope you, too, can see this magnificent creature, but don't count on it.

This ride begins in the "Island City" of Minocqua, a tourist mecca of Wisconsin's Northwoods. A view from the air, or even on a map, shows that Minocqua is surrounded by inland lakes; this ride takes you across and around them on wonderful paved roads and along a portion of a secluded rail-trail, the Bearskin Trail. You begin in tourist central, two blocks off the main drag of the town. The gift, craft, and trinket shops are bustling all summer, and if you're lucky, you might make a sighting even more rare than a bear—Elizabeth Taylor. She owns a hideaway in the area, and rumor has it that she has recently been seen in, of all places, the local fudge shop.

The ride begins two blocks west of Highway 51, in the parking lot behind the post office. Look toward the water to the west and you'll see, at the end of the bridge, an entrance to the Bearskin Trail. This is where you'll come out 30 miles later. You might want to buy your day pass here (self-serve envelopes, $3.00 per day) if you don't have a season pass to use Wisconsin's rail-trails. There's no place to buy a pass where you'll be accessing the trail later in the trip.

Exit the back of the parking lot and head east two blocks to Highway 51 (Oneida Street). Turn left and ride the path/side-

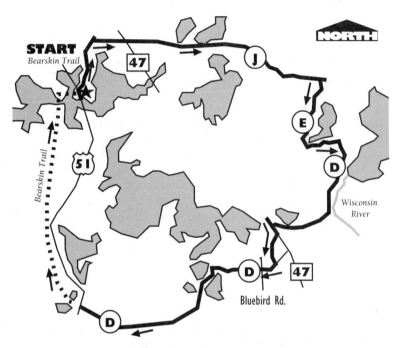

**NORTH**

**START**
*Bearskin Trail*

47

*Bearskin Trail*

51

J

E

D

Wisconsin
River

D

47

Bluebird Rd.

D

**HOW**
**to get**
**there**
From Highway 51
in Minocqua, turn left
at the stoplight onto
Front Street; go two blocks
and turn right into the parking
lot behind the post office.

**DIREC-TIONS**
**at a glance**

0.0  Turn right from the back of the parking lot in Minocqua.

0.2  Turn left onto Highway 51/Oneida Street.

1.6  Turn right onto County J.

2.6  Cross Highway 47.

8.7  Turn right onto County E.

12.5  County E ends; continue straight on County D.

15.4  Turn left onto Highway 47.

15.5  Turn right onto Bluebird Road

16.4  Turn right onto County D.

23.3  Cross Highway 51; turn left in parking lot and walk or ride path to Bearskin Trail.

23.4  Turn right onto Bearskin Trail.

30.3  Return to Minocqua parking lot.

walk to avoid the traffic. Start looking for a place to cross over as the west side of the highway soon runs out of paved path. Once across the highway, ride the path or the road—traffic is at times heavy but there is enough room for bikes—past the turn for Highway 70 to a right onto County J at 1.6 miles. Take comfort in the fact that in just a few miles you'll be out of the traffic, riding through a thick forest and weaving between isolated lakes.

County J is somewhat busy as you make your way out of town, but it has a paved shoulder to Highway 47 at 2.6 miles. Cross Highway 47, where you lose the paved shoulder, and start getting into the fun stuff, the Northern Highlands–American Legion State Forest. After about 4 miles the forest begins closing in, offering just occasional glimpses of a lake to the left. Passing campground turnoffs at 4.8 and 5 miles, there's a nice viewing area of Carol Lake at 5.3 miles. For the next few miles, the road bends and weaves through the forest, rolling up and down through a few hardwoods and more evergreens. Pass Sweeney Lake boat landing at 7.4 miles and turn right onto County E at 8.7 miles.

If you like a twisting, turning road with gently rolling hills, this is a ride for you. Cross a creek at 9.2 miles then enjoy a slight downhill grade. Hug Gilmore Lake to the left, starting at 10.7 miles as you pass around its southern shore, and then swoop along the Rainbow Flowage at 12 miles before coming to a T intersection at 12.5 miles. County E ends, and County D turns left or goes straight—you go straight. The road is new and wider as it swings in a gentle arc to the right, passing along the banks of the Wisconsin River on the left at 13.5 miles. Here the river looks wild and natural, unlike the "working" river of dams and paper mills farther south.

Turn left onto Highway 47 at 15.5 miles. The town of Lake Tomahawk is one block to the right, where you can stop for food, water, and other amenities. Take the next right, just a tenth of a mile after turning, onto Bluebird Road, where you'll find a couple of more challenging (but not long) rolling hills on your way to County D at 16.4 miles. After a right turn onto County D, the road is straight and flat to 17.8 miles until you pass between Carr Lake on the right and McGrath Lake on the left. Ride a ridge between the lakes for the next mile and a half, popping up and down on small hills, before breaking away from the water at around 19.5 miles. The rest of the ride to Highway 54 is flat and dull—but the Bearskin Trail is coming up.

Cross Highway 54 at 23.3 miles and ride into the parking lot of the Pub and Grub (great sandwiches and Friday-night fish fry, by the way). Look to the left and ride or walk up the path a hundred or so yards to the Bearskin Trail. The Bearskin is a crushed-granite trail that follows an abandoned railroad line into Minocqua. It passes through aspens, poplar, birch, cedars, and an occasional maple and oak, with no more than a 3 percent grade. You'll be thankful for the gentle grade just a half mile along the trail as you ride above a lake to the right and a road below to the left.

The trail passes several well-marked roads and a few private-residence driveways. Half a mile south at the Cedar Falls Road crossing, 25.1 miles, will take you to ice cream and food. Just after crossing Timber Ridge Road at 26 miles, where the trail curves slightly to the right, is where I saw the bear. Around 28 miles wetland will appear along the trail on the way to the Kawaga Channel Trestle, which separates two bodies of water, with the town of Minocqua easy to see to the right. Just ahead is the quarter-mile-long bridge that crosses Minocqua Lake, with a bench to rest at and enjoy the view. After crossing the bridge you'll see the parking lot dead ahead.

# Timm's Hill Turnaround

| | |
|---:|:---|
| Number of miles: | 13 |
| Approximate pedaling time: | 1.5 hours |
| Terrain: | Slightly rolling |
| Traffic: | Light on County C; moderate on Highway 86 |
| Things to see: | Ogema; Timm's Hill County Park, with observation towers and Timm's Lake |
| Food: | Ogema; water at the park |

This is the only out-and-back ride in this book. It's a short ride at 13 miles but well worth it, as it swings through the park at Timm's Hill, the highest point in Wisconsin. For many years Rib Mountain, near Wausau, was thought to be the highest point in Wisconsin. A geographical landmark that towers 1,940 feet above the surrounding countryside, Rib at least looks somewhat like a mountain. Surveys in more recent times have shown that Rib is not Wisconsin's highest point; in fact, it's not even the second-highest point. Rib comes in at third place, "dwarfed" by Timm's Hill, which towers 1,951.5 feet above sea level, 11.5 feet higher than Rib. The problem with Timm's Hill is that it merely pokes above surrounding countryside that is already a thousand or so feet above sea level. For instance, Timm's Lake, below the Hill, is at 1,800 feet.

The timber industry swarmed into this area of north-central Wisconsin in the late 1800s, attracted by the white pine, hemlock, and hardwoods. The reach of the railroads into the north soon made Price County the center for lumbering operations. The North Central Railroad came to Ogema in the early 1870s,

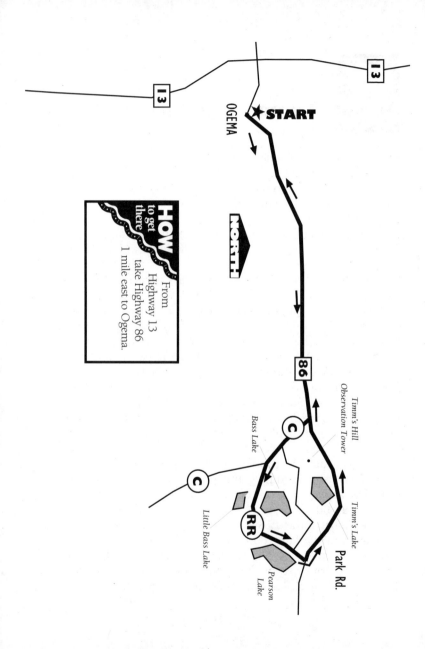

HOW to get there

From Highway 13 take Highway 86 1 mile east to Ogema.

NORTH

OGEMA

START

13

13

86

C

C

RR

Bass Lake

Little Bass Lake

Pearson Lake

Timm's Hill Observation Tower

Timm's Lake

Park Rd.

**DIREC-TIONS at a glance**

0.0  Take Highway 86 east from Ogema.
4.3  Turn right onto County C.
4.8  Go straight onto County Road RR (County C goes right).
6.7  Turn left onto Highway 86.
8.7  Continue past County C.
13.0  Return to Ogema.

and with it came a settlement of Swedish emigrants. A sawmill, a blacksmith's shop, and company houses were established in the Timm's Hill area around the turn of the century. Small timbering operations continued past the heyday of the boom years until 1944, when Timm's Hill was last logged.

The ride begins in Ogema, a small town, which, at present, bears little witness to its once-booming past. Follow Highway 86 east, a gently rolling road with surprisingly little traffic for a state highway. Pass through some farm fields and low trees at 4.3 miles to County C.

After turning right onto County C, passing Timm's Hill Bed and Breakfast, the countryside takes on a distinctly different look—more rustic and tree covered. Sugar maple, ash, basswood, and white birch are the dominant tree species at present. You'll do a bit of climbing before coming to a stop at the junction with County RR at 4.8 miles. County C goes to the right; continue straight on County RR.

County RR is an officially designated state "Rustic Road," one of hundreds singled out for its rural charm as well as low traffic flow. It's a heavily forested, winding road that bobs up and down through a gentle series of roller-coaster hills. Despite being the highest point in Wisconsin, this ride is relatively flat.

At 5 miles, the entrance to Timm's Hill County Park is on the left. Entering the park will take you about a mile to the north end of Bass Lake, a picnic shelter, and access to the walking trails that lead to the observation tower. If you enter here, be sure to come back out the same way for the rest of the ride around County RR.

From the park road County RR passes through a forest, which pushes to the edges of the road, and a marshy area before it comes around the south end of Bass Lake. High Point Village, a small resort, is on the right; across Bass Lake is Timm's Hill. Continuing along County RR, Pearson Lake is on the left, and the other end of Park Road comes out from the left at 5.8 miles. Pass Ring School Road, a dirt road coming in from the left, at 6.1 miles. The road continues weaving its way through the forest to the intersection with Highway 86 at 6.7 miles and then turns to the left.

There are a few curves and gentle hills along Highway 86 as it leads back to Ogema, passing County C (where you went back toward the park) at 8.7 miles. Retrace your route along Highway 86 and you'll be back to Ogema at 13 miles. It's a short ride but definitely worth the time.

# Ginseng Country Tour

| | |
|---:|:---|
| Number of miles: | 25 |
| Approximate pedaling time: | 3 hours |
| Terrain: | Hilly |
| Traffic: | Light |
| Things to see: | Ginseng farms; spectacular scenery; historic buildings of Merrill, including the courthouse; Wisconsin River |
| Food: | In Merrill; Westpahl's Bar at 15.3 miles |

You're in the center of the western half of the Northern Hemisphere with this ride, just a few miles from 45 degrees latitude, 90 degrees longitude. You'll also feel as though you're on top of Wisconsin when you see the incredible views from these rolling hills. The ride begins in Merrill, the seat of Lincoln County, located at the confluence of the Wisconsin and Prairie Rivers. Merrill is a river town, but not in the Mark Twain sense; the Wisconsin River was at the center of the late-1800s logging boom, and Merrill was part of the action. As a result of the rivers, finding your way through Merrill's maze of streets takes a good sense of direction and sharp map-reading skills. While in Merrill, be sure to check out the historic, colonial-style courthouse, completed in 1902. Its 156-foot-high tower makes it easy to find.

The ride begins in the western edge of the city at Ott's Park, located in a residential neighborhood in a bend of the Wisconsin River. The Wausau Wheeler Bicycle Club uses this route, as well as a longer, 65-mile route, as part of an annual metric century

each year in July. Head out of the park a quarter mile to a stop at Highway 64/107. Continue straight on Foster, which somehow turns into Tannery Road. There will be a sign for Tannery Road to the left at about 1 mile, but stay straight until you reach the intersection with Joe Snow Road at 1.3 miles, where you make a left turn. At 1.5 miles turn right onto County I and begin climbing.

Rivers are in valleys, and the Wisconsin River cuts a deep valley in some places. Once you've climbed out of the valley onto the ridges above, you'll be constantly going up and down long, gradual hills. Your reward for climbing will be some breathtaking scenery. As you work your way up County I, take a peek behind you at Merrill below and the countryside to your right. On the day I rode here I saw a brilliant rainbow off to left as I traveled up the hill. The road rolls through farmland until a nice downhill, the first of many, at 4.1 miles. Continue past County FF at 4.5 miles and soon begin another climb.

Look to the left at 5.4 miles—that hillside covered in a latticework of wood is a ginseng farm, the first of many you'll see on this ride. Ginseng, the root of which is believed to have medicinal value, particularly among the Chinese, is found in the wild in shaded forests. These wood structures cover the ginseng, simulating forest conditions. Formerly an oddity, ginseng farms are now popping up all over central Wisconsin, an area that is one of the leading exporters of ginseng to China.

After the ginseng farm enjoy a nice, long downhill through beautiful rolling countryside. There are a few trees sprinkled throughout the cleared farmland, but, for the most part, the view is unencumbered. After another ginseng farm to the left, there's an uphill to a stop at County F. Turn right here, at 6.5 miles, through hilly farmland for some significant gradual climbing. Pass a ginseng farm before Adams Lane at 8.1 miles and then face a pretty stiff uphill to 8.5 miles, followed by some fun up-and-down rolling.

Just past County O at 9.1 miles, look to the left for a view of Rib Mountain near Wausau. Another ginseng farm is just ahead, as well as a spectacular view far off into the distance, and a great

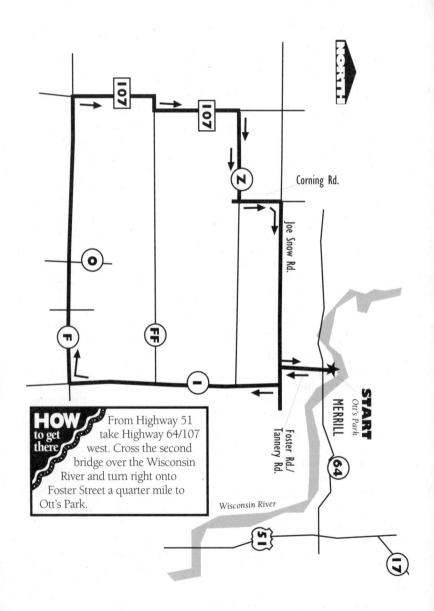

NORTH

107

107

Z

Corning Rd.

O

F

FF

I

Joe Snow Rd.

**HOW**
**to get**
**there**
From Highway 51 take Highway 64/107 west. Cross the second bridge over the Wisconsin River and turn right onto Foster Street a quarter mile to Ott's Park.

**START**
*Ott's Park*
MERRILL

64

Foster Rd./
Tannery Rd.

*Wisconsin River*

51

17

**DIREC-TIONS at a glance**

| | |
|---|---|
| 0.0 | From Ott's Park turn south onto Foster Road. |
| 0.3 | Cross Highway 64/107. |
| 0.8 | Continue past Tannery Road. |
| 1.3 | Turn left onto Joe Snow Road. |
| 1.5 | Turn right onto County I. |
| 2.5 | Continue straight past County Z. |
| 4.5 | Continue past County FF. |
| 6.5 | Turn right turn onto County F. |
| 9.1 | Continue past County O. |
| 12.7 | Turn right onto Highway 107. |
| 14.7 | Turn right onto County FF (still part of Highway 107). |
| 15.3 | Turn left, following Highway 107. |
| 17.0 | Turn right onto County Z. |
| 19.0 | Turn left onto Corning Road. |
| 19.9 | Turn right onto Joe Snow Road. |
| 23.7 | Turn left onto Tannery Road. |
| 24.7 | Cross Highway 64/107. |
| 25.0 | Return to Ott's Park. |

downhill from 9.6 miles to 10 miles; the scenery here is picture-postcard stuff. After another uphill enjoy the ride down at 10.3 miles and be sure to check out the huge ginseng operation on the left. At 10.6 miles cross a creek—a sure sign in central Wisconsin that you'll be climbing soon—and then head up again all the way to 11.7 miles. Take a break at 12.1 miles and check out the abandoned gas station out here in the middle of nowhere, as well as the fantastic 360-degree view spread out before you.

Drop down to Highway 107 at 12.7 miles, turn right, and begin the longest climb of the ride. At 13.8 miles you'll think it's over as it levels off, offering outstanding views, but you'll roll up and up again to 14.5 miles. At 14.7 miles turn right onto County FF, which is still Highway 107; then follow Highway 107 on the next left, at about 15.3 miles. Westpahl's Bar can provide you with refreshments and munchies. A short climb is followed by a very nice downhill. The scenery now becomes more forested, with a few homes and farms dotting the trees. The road levels a bit at 15.9 miles, then gives way to more downhill and a small rise at County Z. Turn right onto County Z through woods and farmland.

At mile 19 turn left onto Corning Road, passing a large dairy farm on the right. Crest a little knob and meet Joe Snow Road at 19.9 miles. Turn right here and enjoy the beautiful forested hills, laced with occasional farm fields to the left. Take your time up this climb to enjoy the view. When you get to the top of Snow Hill at 21 miles, you might stop in the little church and give thanks that the hills are just about over. The top of this ridge provides some of the best scenery of the entire route, with a pleasant downhill run as well. Merrill can be seen off in the distance.

At 22.3 miles the downhill begins to level as you drop back into the river valley. Turn left at 23.7 miles onto Tannery Road, which turns back into Foster, and continue back toward the park. Cross the highway at 24.7 miles, and Ott's Park awaits you at 25 miles.

# Lakewood and the Nicolet National Forest

| | |
|---:|:---|
| Number of miles: | 17.3 |
| Approximate pedaling time: | 2 hours |
| Terrain: | Rolling, with some long hills |
| Traffic: | Moderate on Highway 32; light elsewhere |
| Things to see: | Forest roads, lakes, McCaslin Brook, antiques and craft shops in Lakewood |
| Food: | Lakewood; bar/restaurant at 9.9 miles; various restaurants at 13.7 miles |

Nowhere will you find a better reason for preserving our natural wonders than in the Nicolet National Forest. This is how it was years ago before the lumber barons came in and stripped Wisconsin's Northwoods of its forests. But this is not a preserve, an area completely undisturbed by man; the Nicolet National Forest is managed for timber sale as well as recreation, and selective logging takes place throughout the area. The Forest Service, however, leaves the majority of its charge in an undisturbed, natural state. On this ride you'll get a hint of what it must have been like before European settlers came to Wisconsin.

The forest is named for Jean Nicolet, a French explorer credited with discovering Wisconsin in 1634. Camping, hiking, boating, swimming, cross-country skiing, and bicycling are all popular activities. Begin the ride in Lakewood. Park in the gravel lot just north of County F on Highway 32, across from the Paul Bunyan statue on Main Street. Lakewood is a typical small, northern-Wisconsin tourist town, with restaurants, gal-

leries, gift shops, and antiques stores. Head north 1 mile to a left turn onto Archibald Lake Road, passing Chain Lake to the north. The road follows the lay of the land, rising up and down, weaving around and over ridges and between lakes.

Pass a few residences tucked into the trees and prepare for a deceptively big hill. It doesn't seem to be much at first, but it swings to the left, then up again for nearly a mile. Cathedral Drive goes to the right at 2.4 miles. It's a dirt road, but if it seems hard packed (it can get sloppy at times), take a mile side trip to see one of the few remaining stands of original white pines in Wisconsin. Back on Archibald Lake Road, at 2.9 miles, you'll drop down, winding back and forth through a dense forest. Occasionally glance to the side, through the trees, and see heavily forested small valleys. Enjoy a nice swooping downhill at 4.1 miles; in fact, much of the ride through the forest is gradually downhill after that long climb to start.

At 5.3 miles, past Bass Lake Road to the right, the forest opens up a bit, and the road swings to the right, then down. At 5.8 miles pull into the parking lot for Bass Lake, where you can take a swim. There's also a campground here. Pass Boat Landing Road at 5.9 miles and enter a swampy, marshy area. Stop at 6.4 miles and turn left, still on Archibald Lake Road. The road goes along Boot Lake to the right, following a high ridge, with a wetland and Barnes Lake farther off to the left. You'll be about 25 feet above Boot Lake, with a good view of the pristine little lake. There's some development along the lake, but much of the shore is heavily forested. At 7.5 miles turn right onto County T.

County T climbs gradually but almost constantly for much of the next mile and a half. There isn't a paved shoulder, but there isn't much traffic to worry about on this stretch. You'll soon get off onto a quiet backroad. Turn left onto McCaslin Drive at 9.9 miles, where there's a small bar/restaurant if you're in need of refreshments. McCaslin will swing back to County T a couple of times; if you miss a turn, don't worry; County T will take you back to Highway 32.

Follow McCaslin as it runs down along McCaslin Brook be-

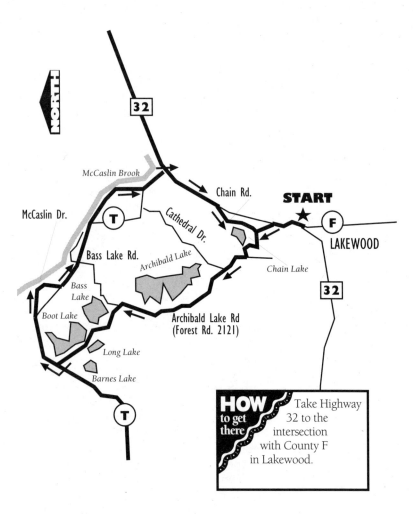

NORTH

**32**

McCaslin Brook

McCaslin Dr.

Chain Rd.

**START**

★

**F**

LAKEWOOD

Cathedral Dr.

**T**

Bass Lake Rd.

Archibald Lake

Chain Lake

**32**

Bass
Lake

Boot Lake

Archibald Lake Rd
(Forest Rd. 2121)

Long Lake

Barnes Lake

**T**

**HOW** to get there  Take Highway
32 to the
intersection
with County F
in Lakewood.

**DIREC-TIONS at a glance**

0.0 Go north on Highway 32 to Lakewood.
1.0 Turn left onto Archibald Lake Road (Forest Road 2121).
2.4 Continue past Cathedral Drive.
5.3 Continue past Bass Lake Road.
6.4 Turn left, continuing on Archibald Lake Road.
7.5 Turn right onto County T.
9.9 Turn left onto McCaslin Drive.
10.8 Turn left onto County T.
11.3 Turn left onto McCaslin Drive.
11.6 Continue right on McCaslin Drive.
11.7 Turn left on McCaslin Drive.
13.0 Turn left onto County T.
13.7 Turn right onto Highway 32.
15.3 Turn right onto Chain Road.
16.3 Turn left onto Archibald Lake Road.
16.4 Turn right onto Highway 32.
17.3 Return to intersection of Highway 32 and County F in Lakewood.

fore coming back to County T at 10.8 miles. Turn left onto T to 11.3 miles and then turn left again onto McCaslin Drive for another good look at the brook. Stop at 11.6 miles, then turn right, followed by a left onto McCaslin Drive just a tenth of a mile up and right before County T. This again follows the brook to 13 miles, where you turn left onto County T. You could, of course, avoid all this turning by simply riding County T, but the various turns onto McCaslin are much more scenic, and there is less traffic.

Turn right onto Highway 32 at 13.7 miles, where there are numerous choices for food and snacks. There is considerably more traffic on Highway 32 but also a bit of a paved shoulder.

Turn right onto Chain Road at 15.3 miles and follow it down past Chain Lake, parallel to Highway 32. There's a good view of the lake at about 16 miles, as the road passes right along its shore. Turn left onto Archibald Lake Road at 16.3 miles; then make a right onto Highway 32. In a mile you'll be back at your waiting car in Lakewood.

# The Crivitz Cruise

| | |
|---:|:---|
| Number of miles: | 25.6 |
| Approximate pedaling time: | 3 hours |
| Terrain: | Rolling, with a few steep hills |
| Traffic: | Light throughout, except for moderate on Highway 141 |
| Things to see: | Crivitz Museum, Lake Nocquebay, wildlife refuge, Rustic Road segment |
| Food: | At the start; Lantow's Resort at 19.7 miles; Mohawk Resort at 21.9 miles |

European settlement in northeast Wisconsin began with the arrival of the first fur traders in the late 1700s, but the real boom times came thirty years later. The dense forests and many rivers became a haven for lumber barons, who took thousands of acres of virgin timber from northern Wisconsin. Rivers were choked with trees that were floated downstream to dozens of waiting sawmills.

The greatest fire disaster in U.S. history occurred on October 8, 1871, to the south of Crivitz in and around Peshtigo. A year-long drought, which had turned forests to tinder, set the stage for a roaring blaze, a tornado of fire that swept across the region, killing more than 1,000 people and wiping out thousands of acres of forest. Little is known about the Great Peshtigo Fire because of a quirk in history—it occurred on the same day as the Great Chicago Fire, which got far more notice in the history books. The far-more-destructive Wisconsin fire is remembered in Peshtigo at the Peshtigo Fire Museum. This ride is near Crivitz, which was barely spared from the ravages of the fire. To

find out more about the lumber barons and early history of Crivitz, visit the Crivitz Area Museum on South Street.

The ride begins at the parking lot for Platter Restaurant/ Hotel and Crivitz Cross Country Ski Center, 1.4 miles north of town on Highway 141, and follows much of one portion of the Tour de Colour, a ride organized to benefit the Marinette County Cross Country Ski Association. Cross Highway 141, head east down Lake Nocquebay Road for a half mile, turn left onto St. Paul Road, and begin a climb into the countryside. The hill crests at 1.2 miles, with good views of rolling hills off in the distance. At 2.3 miles turn left onto Townline Road, down a hill to a right turn onto Highway 141. Highway 141 can be busy, but there is a paved shoulder, and you'll be on the highway for only a half mile. Turn right at the wayside onto East Townline Road at 3.1 miles. There's no road sign here; just look for the wayside and turn right.

This portion of the ride is through a small residential area for the next mile and a half. Pass Sweetheart County Road, at 3.9 miles, to a sharp bend south into a heavily forested area, at 4.9 miles. The terrain changes to gently rolling, with forests and farm fields for scenery. At 5.4 miles turn right onto Pleasant Road for a pleasant and peaceful ride through a rustic, rural area. Although you won't be able to see it, Lake Nocquebay is to the south. Turn left onto Maple Beach Road at 7.1 miles. A right turn here will lead to a resort and the lake about a mile away. Heading away from the lake, pass through a swampy area, cross a creek, and then climb for half a mile before a stop at County X, 8 miles into the ride; turn right onto County X.

County X is a gently rolling, meandering road out into the countryside. The few farms are evidence of the persistence of some people to make a living off the land where many others have failed. At one time nearly one-third of the county had been cleared for farmland, but poor soil and the difficulty of getting products to market from this remote area made most early farmers simply give up and move away. At 10 miles pass Pines Road; then look for a small, older log home to the right. You'll pass an-

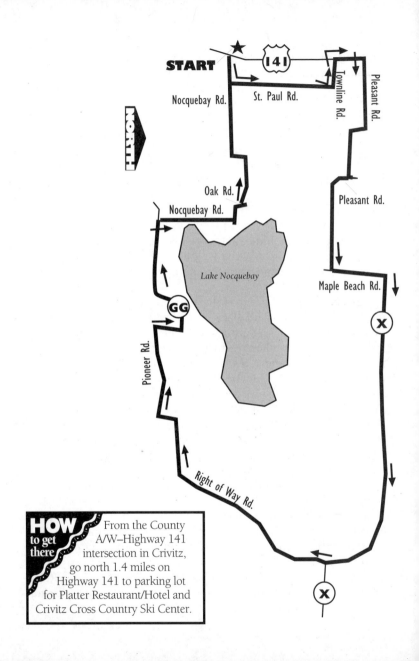

START

US 141

Nocquebay Rd.

St. Paul Rd.

Townline Rd.

Pleasant Rd.

NORTH

Oak Rd.

Nocquebay Rd.

Pleasant Rd.

Lake Nocquebay

Maple Beach Rd.

GG

X

Pioneer Rd.

Right of Way Rd.

X

**HOW to get there** From the County A/W–Highway 141 intersection in Crivitz, go north 1.4 miles on Highway 141 to parking lot for Platter Restaurant/Hotel and Crivitz Cross Country Ski Center.

**DIREC-TIONS**
**at a glance**

| | |
|---|---|
| 0.0 | From the parking lot cross Highway 141 to Nocquebay Road. |
| 0.4 | Turn left onto St. Paul Road. |
| 2.3 | Turn left onto Townline Road. |
| 2.7 | Turn right onto Highway 141. |
| 3.1 | Turn right at wayside onto East Townline Road (no sign). |
| 5.4 | Turn right onto Pleasant Road. |
| 7.1 | Turn left onto Maple Beach Road. |
| 8.0 | Turn right onto County X. |
| 13.2 | Turn right onto Right of Way Road. |
| 13.3 | Stay right as an unnamed road comes in from left. |
| 16.1 | Stay right as another unnamed road comes in from left. |
| 17.4 | Turn right onto Pioneer Road. |
| 18.8 | Turn right onto County GG. |
| 21.4 | Turn right onto Nocquebay Road. |
| 22.6 | Turn left onto Oak Road/Nocquebay Road. |
| 25.6 | Cross Highway 141 to parking lot. |

other log home at 11.5 miles before County X takes a long, sweeping turn to the right. At 13.2 County X veers left; turn right here onto Right of Way Road.

This is the most spectacular portion of the ride, a long, gentle downhill through a dense tunnel of trees. Adjacent to a state wildlife refuge and Marinette County Forest land, the road was originally part of the Wisconsin-Michigan Railroad. It is also an officially designated Rustic Road, a program identifying lightly traveled roads with outstanding natural features. With the thick forest around the road, there's little wonder why this route is chosen for the fall Tour de Colour Bike Ride.

The road meanders south and west on a gentle downhill grade to 15.5 miles, where the forest opens up. At 16.1 miles all that remains of the LeRoy Logging Camp Store and Dancehall,

1903–1913, is a sign indicating where it formerly stood. A road (no sign) comes in from the left just past this point. Stay to the right here. Another unmarked road comes in from the left at 16.3; again, stay to the right.

Turn right onto Pioneer Road at 17.4 miles. The road surface is rough here but you'll be on it only for about a mile. Turn right onto County GG at 18.8, a much-improved road. You're now south of Lake Nocquebay and heading north toward the lake. At 19.2 miles County GG veers to the left, with the lake visible to the right. Lantow's Resort, with access to the lake, is at 19.7 miles. The road swings south, then east, to the right, and back into farm country.

Turn right onto Lake Nocquebay Road at 21.4 miles and head back toward the lake, passing Mohawk Resort at 21.9 miles. Cross a bridge where a creek flows from the lake that feeds the Peshtigo River—this is a good place to view the lake—to Oak Road/Lake Nocquebay Road, at 22.6 miles. Turn left here and begin climbing up and away from the lake. After the climb the road winds and rolls alternately through fields and forest. Pass St. Paul Road on the right, at 25.2 miles; then come back to Highway 141 and the parking lot at 25.6 miles.

# Death's Door to Washington Island

| | |
|---:|:---|
| Number of miles: | 14.7 |
| Approximate pedaling time: | 1.5 hours |
| Terrain: | Flat to rolling |
| Traffic: | Light |
| Things to see: | Ferry crossing, Detroit Harbor; West Harbor; School House Beach, Washington Harbor; Mountain Park Lookout |
| Food: | At the ferry dock; Main Road at 5.2 miles; Detroit Harbor Road and Lobdell Point Road at 13 miles |

Depending on the weather, you'll either enjoy the half-hour, 6-mile crossing from the Door County peninsula to Washington Island or wonder whatever in the world made you attempt such foolishness. When the wind whips across the channel, known as Porte des Mortes (Death's Door), and the little car ferry bobs in the wind and waves, you'll have a firsthand idea of why this stretch of water has claimed many a life through the years. Between 1837 and 1914 twenty-four vessels were lost at Death's Door, and another forty were lost in the nearby islands. Although a rough crossing might make you nervous, be comforted in the fact that the car ferries don't run if the crossing is dangerous.

Washington Island has about 650 year-round residents and relies heavily on the tourist trade. In the summer months the island's population swells to several thousand. Fishing is still an

important industry for islanders, many of whom are descendants of Icelandic settlers who came to the island in the 1800s.

From the ferry dock pass the terminal to a left turn onto Green Bay Road. This quiet, tree-lined road swings around Lobdell's Point, passing some stately lakefront homes, including an interesting rough-cut log home at 1.3 miles. The terrain is gentle, and the road comes close to the lake at several points. Turn left at 2.3 miles onto Lobdell Point Road. There's no street sign, but there is a stop sign. Lobdell Point Road winds its way through the forest on new pavement with a bike lane. At 2.9 miles turn left onto Old West Harbor Road, a beautiful road through a dense forest.

The little community of West Harbor sits on the edge of a bay at 3.7 miles. Turn right onto West Harbor Road at 4.1 miles for a gradual climb through gently rolling terrain into farm fields like those found everywhere else in Wisconsin. At 4.7 miles turn left onto Main Road, a designated bike route with a paved shoulder. Just after 5 miles there are some restaurants and a food store. Turn right onto Jackson Harbor Road at 6.5 miles. A side trip to the Jacobsen Museum, which houses a collection of natural and historical artifacts from the island, is straight ahead one-tenth of a mile, then left for 1.8 miles. If you go to the museum, keep in mind that the road is uphill coming back.

After the right turn onto Jackson Harbor Road, the entrance to School House Beach is on the left at 6.7 miles at Washington Harbor. St. Michael's Chapel is across the road from the beach entrance. There are some gift shops along here, a few houses, and a farm museum that is housed in a number of log buildings just past 7 miles. Turn right at 8 miles onto Mountain Road. To get to Jackson Harbor and the ferry crossing to Rock Island State Park, continue straight for 2 miles. Rock Island State Park, which comprises all of the small island, has camping, hiking trails, and a beach. No vehicles, including bikes, are allowed on the island.

Mountain Road leads to Mountain Lookout Park and its 183-step tower, which offers a stunning view of Green Bay, Lake

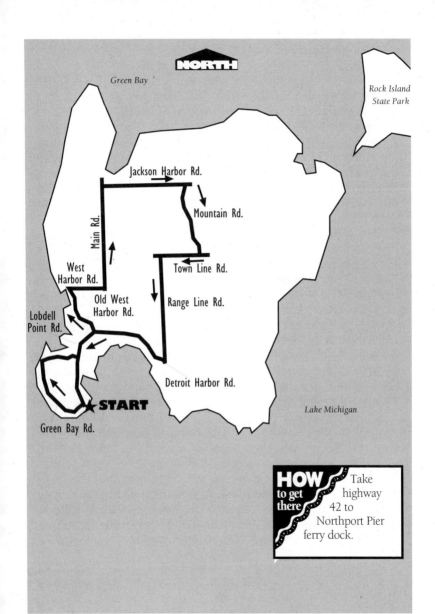

NORTH

Green Bay

Rock Island
State Park

Jackson Harbor Rd.

Mountain Rd.

Main Rd.

West
Harbor Rd.

Town Line Rd.

Old West
Harbor Rd.

Range Line Rd.

Lobdell
Point Rd.

Detroit Harbor Rd.

★ START

Lake Michigan

Green Bay Rd.

**HOW** to get there  Take highway 42 to Northport Pier ferry dock.

**DIREC-TIONS at a glance**

0.0 Start at the ferry dock on Washington Island.

0.1 Turn left onto Green Bay Road.

2.3 Turn left onto Lobdell Point Road (no sign).

2.9 Turn left onto Old West Harbor Road.

4.1 Turn right onto West Harbor Road.

4.7 Turn left onto Main Road.

6.5 Turn right onto Jackson Harbor Road.

8.0 Turn right onto Mountain Road.

9.3 Turn right onto Town Line Road.

10.0 Turn left onto Range Line Road.

11.7 Turn right onto Detroit Harbor Road.

13.0 Continue straight onto Lobdell Point Road.

14.7 Return to ferry dock.

Michigan, and the surrounding islands. Slide around the park for a gentle downhill to a right turn onto Town Line Road. Turn left onto Range Line Road at 10 miles, pass a Christmas farm on the left, and then roll through a series of small hills. Continue past Lake View Road at 11 miles and head toward Detroit Harbor.

Turn right onto Detroit Harbor Road at 11.7 miles, horseshoe around the harbor to the left, and stop at 13 miles where you'll find a post office and restaurants. Continue straight onto Lobdell Point Road and follow it as it weaves down through trees back toward the ferry dock. You pass Green Bay Road at 13.7 miles and reach the dock at 14.7 miles.

# Crossing Door Shore to Shore

|  |  |
|---|---|
| Number of miles: | 25.9 |
| Approximate pedaling time: | 3 hours |
| Terrain: | Rolling |
| Traffic: | Light in the country; moderate through Fish Creek and Baileys Harbor |
| Things to see: | Baileys Harbor, Peninsula State Park, Fish Creek, Lake Michigan, and Green Bay |
| Food: | Baileys Harbor, Fish Creek, Peninsula Center |

The Door County peninsula, jutting into Lake Michigan and forming Green Bay to the west, has long been one of Wisconsin's most popular tourist destinations. It's so popular that a bike ride might be best in spring or fall or at least midweek during summer; the hordes of visitors can make biking difficult on summer weekends. One nice thing about Door County in summer is that the lake breezes that blow across the peninsula provide a natural air conditioning, making steamy summer days bearable for bike riders.

Start in Baileys Harbor on the Lake Michigan side, at the intersection of Highway 57 and County F. There's a parking area across from County F behind the mini-mart, along the bay. There also is a lot right behind the visitor center on County F, just up from Highway 57.

The Lake Michigan–side towns are not as congested as the

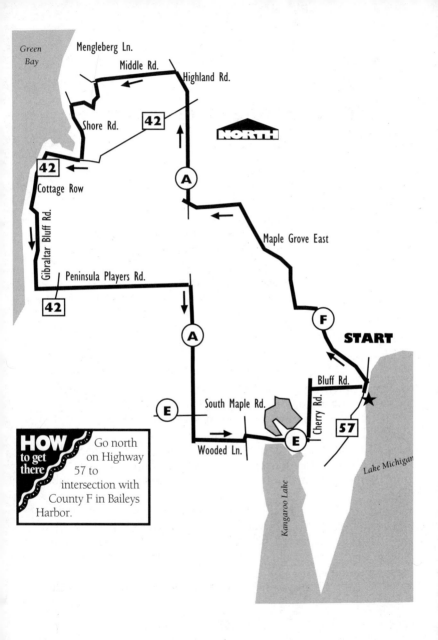

Green
Bay

Mengleberg Ln.

Middle Rd.

Highland Rd.

Shore Rd.

**42**

**NORTH**

Ⓐ

**42** ←

Cottage Row

Maple Grove East

Gibraltar Bluff Rd.

Peninsula Players Rd.

**42**

Ⓐ

Ⓕ

**START**

Bluff Rd.

Ⓔ

South Maple Rd.

Ⓔ

Cherry Rd.

**57**

★

Wooded Ln.

**HOW** to get there
Go north on Highway 57 to intersection with County F in Baileys Harbor.

Kangaroo Lake

Lake Michigan

| | |
|---|---|
| 0.0 | Go north on Highway 57 to County F in Baileys Harbor. |
| 1.0 | Turn left onto County F. |
| 4.4 | Turn left onto Maple Grove East (County F). |
| 5.5 | Turn right onto County A. |
| 7.3 | Cross Highway 42 to Highland Road, Peninsula State Park. |
| 7.9 | Turn left onto Middle Road. |
| 10.0 | Turn left onto Mengleberg Lane. |
| 10.5 | Turn left onto Shore Road (no sign). |
| 11.7 | Turn right onto Highway 42 through Fish Creek. |
| 12.2 | Continue straight onto Main Street (Highway 42 goes left). |
| 12.3 | Turn left onto Cottage Row. |
| 13.9 | Turn right onto Gibraltar Bluff Road. |
| 14.6 | Continue straight onto Orchard Road. |
| 15.3 | Turn left onto Peninsula Players Road. |
| 17.7 | Cross Highway 42. |
| 18.3 | Turn right onto County A. |
| 20.7 | Cross County E at Peninsula Center. |
| 21.2 | Turn left onto Wooded Lane. |
| 22.2 | Turn left onto South Maple Road. |
| 22.3 | Turn right onto County E. |
| 23.5 | Turn left onto Cherry Road (sign obscured by brush). |
| 24.5 | Turn right onto Bluff Road. |
| 25.6 | Turn left onto Highway 57. |
| 25.9 | Return to County F in Baileys Harbor. |

bay-side towns, but they still provide a bit of an old-time fishing-village atmosphere. Head north on County F up and away from the town, stop at 1 mile, and then turn left, still on County F. Signs along the road indicate this is a designated bike route.

By 1.5 miles the worst of the climbing is over, and you enter some fairly typical Wisconsin farm country, although little galleries and unique gift shops seem to pop up at the strangest places in Door County. Pass a country church at 3.2 miles and then come to a stop at 4.4 miles. Turn left here onto Maple Grove East, which is still County F. At 5.5 miles turn right onto County A and follow this down to a stop at Highway 42 at 7.3 miles. Carefully cross the highway onto Highland Road and enter Peninsula State Park.

Peninsula State Park, nestled on the shore of Green Bay, is Wisconsin's largest and most popular state park. The roads through the park alone would make a great bike ride. Turn left onto Middle Road at 7.9 miles. This is a beautiful, narrow, forested road that cuts a serpentine path across the park. At 10 miles begin a good downhill to the right, then left; stay left onto Mengleberg Lane as Middle Road goes right. Stop at 10.5 miles for a left turn onto Shore Road, although there's no sign here indicating it is Shore Road. There's a nice spot to view the lake at 11.1 miles, with Fish Creek across the bay. Pass the park headquarters (bathrooms and beverages) at 11.4 miles; then turn right onto Highway 42 at 11.7 miles. For a small town Fish Creek can have one heck of a traffic problem. Work your way through town, passing an array of restaurants, hotels, galleries, boutiques, and gift shops. Highway 42 turns left at 12.2 miles, but go straight here. At 12.3 miles turn left onto Cottage Row.

The row of "cottages" you'll pass are homes of opulent splendor along the water's edge, with a high bluff to your left. Stone fences line the tree-lined road, adding an exclusive air to this quiet neighborhood. At 13.6 miles swing left and up the ridge. This is an intense little climb, with a switchback halfway up, but it's over at 13.9 miles, where you turn right onto Gibraltar Bluff Road. Follow along as the road rolls up and down and then continue straight onto Orchard Road at 14.6 miles. Stop at 15.3 miles for a left turn onto Peninsula Players Road, although there isn't a street sign to guide you.

Cross Highway 42 at 15.7 miles and continue on Peninsula

Players Road uphill to 16 miles, where you'll enjoy a nice down-hill through farm fields. Turn right onto County A at 18.3 miles and follow the gently rolling road south, passing County EE at 19.7 miles, then coming to a stop at County E, at 20.7 miles, and the small community of Peninsula Center, where there's a small store and a tavern. Go straight to a left turn onto Wooded Lane at 21.2 miles. Just when you begin to enjoy a downhill run, you'll stop at South Maple Lane, 22.2 miles. Turn left here to a right onto County E at 22.3 miles.

County E passes between Kangaroo Lake, a large inland lake to the right, and small Mud Lake to the left. The Coyote Road House, with food and beverages, is just before the lake crossing. On the other side of the lakes, at 23.5 miles, turn left onto Cherry Street; the sign is hidden by brush. Climb up to 23.5 miles, pass Summit Road at 24 miles, and then turn right onto Bluff Road at 24.5 miles. A pleasant tree-lined road, Bluff Road will take you over a couple of small hills and back into Baileys Harbor on a downhill that comes to stop at Highway 57, at 25.6 miles. Just across the highway is an inviting ice-cream shop. Turn left and ride through Baileys Harbor, coming back to County F at 25.9 miles.

A nice side trip would be to the Ridges Sanctuary, a 1,100-acre preserve and nature center just outside Baileys Harbor. The sanctuary sponsors an annual bike ride across Door County, usually in June.

# A Dip by the Eau Claire Dells

| | |
|---:|:---|
| **Number of miles:** | 14.8 |
| **Approximate pedaling time:** | 1.5 hours |
| **Terrain:** | Slightly rolling |
| **Traffic:** | Light |
| **Things to see:** | Dells of the Eau Claire River, ginseng farms, Eau Claire River wetlands |
| **Food:** | Water at the park |

The placid Eau Claire River, which flows into the Wisconsin River, cascades over a series of limestone outcroppings 15 miles east of Wausau in central Wisconsin. Marathon County has built a beautiful park—Eau Claire River Dells County Park—at a site that is virtually in the middle of nowhere. There are no towns nearby, and the countryside is given over to farmland. The park is the rare kind of place that seems known only to locals— which is all the better for visitors. Just below the bridge at County Highway Y, the river, not more than a wide stream at this point, flows through, over, and around a staircase of rough bluffs. Upstream, just across County Y, there are camping facilities and a beach. The park has playgrounds, hiking trails, bathrooms, shelters, and drinking water. Eau Claire Dells is an accessible place where you can wander out into the river onto the rocks and watch the water rush below. It is also a dangerous place that has claimed the lives of several people who have ignored warnings not to dive or swim in the rapids. Heed the warnings.

The ride begins at the upper parking lot north of the river off County Y. Used as a ride sponsored by the Wausau Wheelers

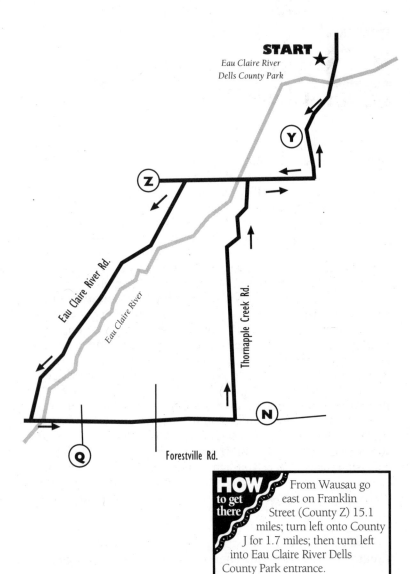

START
*Eau Claire River*
*Dells County Park*

Y

Z

Eau Claire River Rd.

*Eau Claire River*

Thornapple Creek Rd.

N

Q

Forestville Rd.

**HOW** to get there   From Wausau go east on Franklin Street (County Z) 15.1 miles; turn left onto County J for 1.7 miles; then turn left into Eau Claire River Dells County Park entrance.

**DIREC-TIONS**
**at a glance**

| | |
|---|---|
| 0.0 | Turn right onto County Y from the Eau Claire River Dells County Park entrance. |
| 1.7 | Turn right onto County Z. |
| 2.4 | Cross Eau Claire River. |
| 3.2 | Turn left onto Eau Claire River Road. |
| 6.8 | Turn left onto County N. |
| 7.3 | Continue past County Q to the right. |
| 8.3 | Continue past Forestville Road. |
| 9.3 | Turn left onto Thornapple Creek Road. |
| 12.7 | Turn right onto County Z. |
| 13.2 | Turn left onto County Y. |
| 14.8 | Return to entrance to Eau Claire Dells County Park. |

Bike Club, there might even be road markings on this route to guide you. Turn right (south) onto County Y and drop down to cross the river. Traffic is usually light, so you can stop and look right down the dells to the rocky outcropping on the left. Getting up from the river requires a bit of a climb, but nothing strenuous.

A few evergreens and some hardwoods give way to farmers' fields and then, at nine-tenths of a mile, a ginseng farm to the left. Ginseng, a root crop favored by the Chinese for its medicinal value, is grown throughout central Wisconsin. The plants are found naturally on the forest floor, and farmers simulate forest cover by building an elaborate wood lattice over the plants. After a slight climb enjoy a mostly downhill cruise to County Z at 1.7 miles. Turn right onto County Z, where the forest closes in a bit, speckled by an occasional residence, then drops to cross the river at 2.4 miles. Here the Eau Claire looks completely tame, giving no hint of the dells just 1 or 2 miles upriver. After a half-mile climb up from the river, glance back to see the rolling hills of central Wisconsin and feel blessed that this ride does not include those hills.

At 3.2 miles turn left to follow the river on Eau Claire River Road. The scenery opens up more here, with some scrub trees, before a gentle downhill that curves to the right. The views are of more hills off in the distance. As the road curves back to the left, the slight river valley is obvious on the left. At 5.4 miles there are ginseng farms on both sides of the road; the one on the left gives an up-close view of the tender plants beneath the wooden framework.

Eau Claire River Road follows the gently twisting flow of the river, putting you right on the riverbanks between 6.2 miles and the left turn onto County N at 6.8. The rusty bridge might not instill confidence, but it is safe. A slight climb up from the river offers another good view of the hilly countryside over cleared farm fields. The road rolls slightly to a left turn onto Thornapple Creek Road at 9.3 miles, where you're greeted with a slight climb. The payoff is yet another nice view of the rolling hills before a gradual downhill, beginning at 9.6 miles, which flattens out as it passes occasional small farms. A pleasant coasting downhill at 10.8 miles leads through some scrub brush and across a small creek, a marsh to the left, and then a quick right/left turn combination. The river is visible again, to the left here, before coming back to County Z.

Turn right onto County Z at 12.7 miles, come up from the river, and then dip down to a left turn onto County Y at 13.2 miles. From here retrace the mile and a quarter back to the park entrance—this time riding up the nice cruise that brought you down to the intersection in the first place. If you didn't do it before you left, spend some time walking around the park and along the river. This is special place, off the beaten tourist track, spectacular yet uncrowded. Enjoy.

# River City Ramble

| | |
|---:|:---|
| Number of miles: | 18.1 |
| Approximate pedaling time: | 2 hours |
| Terrain: | Flat |
| Traffic: | Moderate through Wisconsin Rapids; light elsewhere |
| Things to see: | Lake Wazeecha and South Wood County Park, Wisconsin Rapids, Wisconsin River, Consolidated Paper Mill |
| Food: | Water at the park, food throughout Wisconsin Rapids and at Biron; several inns along the route |

Nekoosa, a small town just south of Wisconsin Rapids, is a Winnebago Indian word meaning "running waters," which is what settlers found here in the early 1800s. The first sawmill in the area opened south of Nekoosa in 1833. By 1837 a wood-pulp paper mill was established in Wisconsin Rapids, and the paper industry has been a mainstay of the local economy ever since. To find out more, visit the South Wood County Historical Museum on Third Street South.

Wisconsin Rapids—just "Rapids" to the locals—is a thriving mill town nestled on both sides of the Wisconsin River. There are several fine restaurants; the Alexander House, with art exhibits, and even a municipal zoo. The ride starts to the southeast of the city at South Wood County Park on Lake Wazeecha. There are park roads and entrances on both the north and south sides of the lake; start from the east parking lot on the south side.

The park, a popular place for the locals in the summer months, has all the usual amenities: beaches, playgrounds, toilets, water, boat landings, and camping facilities. Turn right out of the parking lot onto South Park Road. Just before 64th Street at a half mile, pass by another park entrance. Turn left onto 64th Street; then, less than a quarter mile down, turn right onto White Rock Road. This road—in fact, the entire ride—is flat, with hardly a bump anywhere to indicate elevation. Pass through a residential area, with a small Christmas tree farm off to the left at 1.4 miles. Turn right onto 48th Street at 1.7 miles, where you'll come into a wooded area, encounter a slight hill, then get into suburban Wisconsin Rapids. Turn left onto Lake Wazeecha Road at 2.5 miles, then left onto Lake Avenue at 2.8 miles.

After making the turn peer through the trees to the left for a view of an ostrich farm, where you might see some of the huge creatures. The road here is a wide designated bike route, indicated by green and white signs. At 4.5 miles Lake Avenue blends into Chestnut Street, which comes in from the right. If you want a break, you can stop at the Settlement Tavern on the corner here. At 4.8 miles turn right onto 16th Street and you'll pass through residential Wisconsin Rapids. Cross Peach Street at 5 miles and Baker Street at 5.4 miles. Here you might want to stop at the Dairy Bar, a local landmark, for a cone or a shake. Turn left onto Apricot Street at 5.6 miles and continue passing through a residential area. The road bends to the right, but stay on Apricot to the river at 6.2 miles. Turn right onto North First Street.

The buildings you see in front of you are part of Consolidated Papers, one of the large paper companies active in the area. The street, which stays tight to the water, offers some nice views of this portion of the placid Wisconsin River as it passes through a residential area with an occasional stately old riverfront home. At around 8 miles North First Street becomes South Biron Drive as the residential area gives way to more peaceful river country. At 8.5 miles the road swings to the right, away

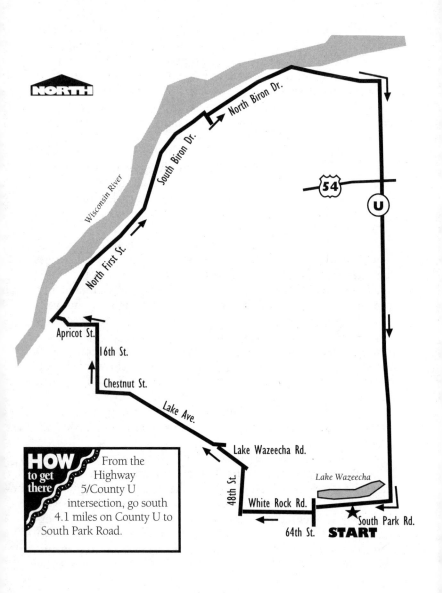

NORTH

Wisconsin River

North Biron Dr.

South Biron Dr.

North First St.

54

U

Apricot St.

16th St.

Chestnut St.

Lake Ave.

Lake Wazeecha Rd.

48th St.

Lake Wazeecha

White Rock Rd.

South Park Rd.

64th St.

★ START

**HOW to get there**
From the Highway 5/County U intersection, go south 4.1 miles on County U to South Park Road.

**DIREC-TIONS at a glance**

| | |
|---|---|
| 0.0 | From South Wood County Park, turn right onto South Park Road. |
| 0.5 | Turn left onto 64th Street. |
| 0.7 | Turn right onto White Rock Road. |
| 1.7 | Turn right onto 48th Street. |
| 2.5 | Turn left onto Lake Wazeecha Road. |
| 2.8 | Turn left onto Lake Avenue. |
| 4.5 | Continue on Lake Avenue as it becomes Chestnut Street. |
| 4.8 | Turn right onto 16th Street |
| 5.6 | Turn left onto Apricot Street. |
| 5.9 | Continue past 11th Street. |
| 6.2 | Turn right onto North First Street. |
| 8.0 | North First Street becomes South Biron Drive. |
| 8.9 | Turn left onto North Biron Drive. |
| 12.1 | Turn right onto County U. |
| 13.5 | Continue past Highway 54 on County U. |
| 17.6 | Turn right onto South Park Road. |
| 18.1 | Return to South Wood County Park entrance. |

from the river, and passes through mountains of logs stacked along the sides of railroad tracks at 8.8 miles. These logs are processed into paper products to become, among other things, books like the one you're holding now.

Turn left at 8.9 miles onto North Biron Road; South Biron Road will take you into the community of Biron a half mile away. Pass the Consolidated Papers R&D facility and, to the left, you'll ride along a concrete retaining wall that obscures your view of the river for about a mile. Once you get past the wall, the river is much wider, much more like a lake. At 10.3 miles there's a cranberry bog to the right.

At 11 miles more homes appear to the right, with occasional boat docks jutting into the river to your left. The road sticks close to the banks as you come up on the setting for the Aqua Skiers Ski Show, with a jumping ramp off shore at 11.8 miles. Parking and boat launching access is at 12 miles, just before a stop sign and a right turn onto County U.

County U is straight and flat all the way back to the park. Scenery alternates between forests and fields, with more of the latter. Cross Highway 54 at 13.5 miles and the Kellner International Bar and Grill at 16.2 miles. Cross County FF/W at 16.8 miles and then turn right onto South Park Road at 17.6 miles. The park entrance is at 18.1 miles. If you have the time, turn right onto North Park Road—just before South Park Road—and explore the north side of the lake before heading back to the parking lot on the south side.

# Hartman Creek/Chain O' Lakes Cruise

| | |
|---:|:---|
| **Number of miles:** | 12.5 |
| **Approximate pedaling time:** | 1.5 hours |
| **Terrain:** | Gentle, with a few rolling hills |
| **Traffic:** | On summer and holiday weekends, moderately heavy but slow-paced in the immediate Lakes area; light midweek |
| **Things to see:** | Hartman Creek State Park; Whispering Pines State Park; Crystal River; chain of twenty-seven connected lakes; antiques; arts, and gift shops; waterfront restaurants; boat rides on the lakes; motorboat and canoe rentals |
| **Food:** | At County Q channel crossing, village of King, two mini-marts on County Q |

Hartman Creek is one of Wisconsin's busiest state parks, and the nearby Chain O' Lakes is one of the state's most popular tourism destinations—a double-edged sword that might make a bicyclist think the area is too crowded for quiet riding. Yet, even on the busiest summer holiday weekends, bicyclists will find just moderate and slow-paced traffic that allows for hours of quiet riding through this scenic area. The reason? This is a land of summer homes, with few lakeside resorts and motels to attract transient weekend tourists. (A few cottages are available at the lakes, one B&B is along the route, and nearby Waupaca offers plenty of hotel/motel rooms.)

The ride begins at Hartman Creek State Park, worth exploring for its swimming and fishing lakes, hiking and mountain-bike trails, and numerous campgrounds. A right turn leads down Rural Road, an officially designated Wisconsin State Rustic Road, noted for its scenic beauty and quiet pastoral charm. After dipping over Hartman Creek and crossing a hiking trail that connects Hartman Creek State Park to the much smaller Whispering Pines State Park (a day park—no camping), the left turn onto Whispering Pines Road leads into the Chain O' Lakes.

"In all the world no lakes like these!" claim the brochures. Although the claim might be local tourism hyperbole, it serves as an introduction to a heavily wooded, winding set of roadways that go past small lakes, ringed by year-round and summer homes. Views of the lakes await around nearly every corner, and a round of miniature golf can be played just a mile down from the Rural Road turnoff. Lakeside homes range from the basic to the elegant—be sure to check out the new Victorian-style home on the right just across the channel past the miniature golf course.

At 3 miles County Q crosses the next channel at the "Indian Crossing," which separates the lakes of the Upper and Lower Chain. A hub of action, the crossing is home to a marina, Ding's Dock (the starting point for Crystal River canoe trips), the Casino (an old-time dance hall that at one time hosted everything from the Big Bands to the Beach Boys), the Wheelhouse (an elegantly rustic bar/restaurant featuring pizza, sandwiches, and occasional live music on the outside deck), and Scooper's Ice Cream Parlour.

From County Q Cleghorn Road leads back onto gently rolling, wooded roads past more of the secluded lakes. Although homes perch on what seems like every inch of shoreline, most of the traffic is on the lakes, not the narrow winding roads. (A left on Country Lane leads to the multitiered Art Barn, an antiques and craft shop.) Farther along on Cleghorn Road, before the Highway 22 intersection, you'll pass more antiques, furniture, and wilderness-print shops on the left.

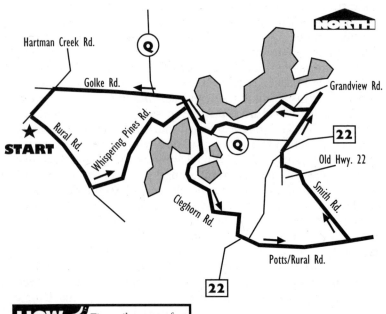

**NORTH**

Hartman Creek Rd.

Golke Rd.

Q

Grandview Rd.

Rural Rd.

**START**

Whispering Pines Rd.

22

Old Hwy. 22

Smith Rd.

Cleghorn Rd.

22

Potts/Rural Rd.

**HOW** to get there
Five miles west of Waupaca on Highway 54, turn south on Hartman Creek Road and proceed 1.6 miles to park entrance.

**DIREC-TIONS at a glance**

| | |
|---|---|
| 0.0 | From the entrance of Hartman Creek Park, turn right onto Rural Road. |
| 0.5 | Cross Hartman Creek. |
| 1.0 | Turn left onto Whispering Pines Road. |
| 1.6 | Continue past entrance to Whispering Pines State Park. |
| 2.8 | Turn right onto County Q. |
| 3.1 | Turn right onto Cleghorn Road. |
| 4.6 | Cross Highway 22. |
| 4.9 | Continue straight on Cleghorn Road; cross bridge over Crystal River. |
| 5.0 | Turn right onto Potts (Rural) Road. |
| 6.3 | Turn left onto Smith Road. |
| 7.5 | Turn right onto Old Highway 22. |
| 7.6 | Cross Highway 22. |
| 8.5 | Turn left onto Grandview Road (continue straight 1.5 miles to business district). |
| 9.9 | Turn right onto County Q. |
| 11.2 | County Q turns right; continue straight on Golke Road. |
| 12.1 | Turn left on Hartman Creek Road. |
| 12.5 | Return to entrance to Hartman Creek Park at Rural Road. |

Crossing Highway 22 leads into the community of Rural at 5 miles, a National Register Historic District of restored homes along the Crystal River that reflects turn-of-the-century architecture. The entire community is on two parallel streets just a couple of blocks long; take a detour and look around. The ride crosses the Crystal River twice, the first time in Rural at 5.1 miles. Rural is a great place to stop and watch the paddlers portage tiny fiberglass canoes. At the turnoff onto Smith Road, at 6.3 miles, the paddlers negotiate a slight rapids, providing ample amusement for the land-locked bicyclist.

After a steady climb on Smith Road, just a little more than a mile of a gradual uphill, you'll cross Highway 22 and begin to enter King. Traffic here picks up slightly until the intersection with Grandview Road at mile 8.5. The collection of buildings ahead on the left are the grounds of the Wisconsin Veterans Home. For food, antiques, and gift shops, pass Grandview Road and continue on for a mile and a half. The Clearwater Harbor Bar and Restaurant, which has a nice waterfront deck overlooking Taylor Lake, offers boat rides—one a paddle wheeler—on the lakes.

Back on Grandview Road a slight quarter-mile climb provides a nice overview of Rainbow Lake, Government Island, and the Veterans Home. At 9.9 miles you're back on County Q for another ride across the Indian Crossing, then back into the countryside. Be sure to go straight on Golke Road at 11.2 miles, where County Q takes a sharp turn to the right. From Golke Road you have a pleasant ride through rural countryside back to Hartman Creek State Park.

# Escaping the Escarpment

| | |
|---:|:---|
| **Number of miles:** | 23.7 |
| **Approximate pedaling time:** | 2.5 hours |
| **Terrain:** | Slightly to moderately rolling |
| **Traffic:** | Light |
| **Things to see:** | Chilton, South Branch of the Manitowoc River, Lake Winnebago, Niagara Escarpment, Stockbridge, Ledge View Nature Center |
| **Food:** | Chilton; Stockbridge at 14.3 miles |

At one time the area between Lake Winnebago and Lake Michigan was covered in a pine forest. After the forest was logged out, fertile agricultural land remained. There are few trees left nowadays, just mile after mile of farm fields, rimmed by occasional tree lines. This ride wanders from Chilton and heads down the Niagara Escarpment through farm country to some great panoramic views of Lake Winnebago. The Niagara Escarpment is a dense, limestone outcropping that runs for more than 1,000 miles from Niagara Falls into Wisconsin east of Lake Winnebago; Chilton sits atop its eastern rim.

Start at Leahy Lions Park on the South Branch of the Manitowoc River just south of downtown Chilton. From the park turn right onto West Main Street; then take the next left onto South State Street/County F. Pass St. Augustine's, a beautiful brick church on the left. Continue straight on West Main Street, and, a half mile later, you're out of town and into the rural countryside.

Where County F turns left, stay straight on West Main Street, pass McHugh Road at 1.6 miles, and then ride up a slight grade before two 90-degree turns—first left, then right. Turn right

onto County BB at 2.8 miles and begin a gradual uphill. Look to the right for a nice view almost to Lake Michigan. Turn left onto Hickory Hills Road at 3.3 miles for a series of gentle downhills to a right onto Twain Road at 4.5 miles. Cross County E at 5.5 miles; then turn left onto Moore Road at 6.2 miles.

The entire ride takes place in rolling farm country, passing fields of corn and occasional fields of brilliant sunflowers. At 7.3 miles turn right onto Long Road for a series of little hills. At 8.4 miles turn left onto Hill Road—a road that owns up to its name—and begin a gradual rolling climb to a nice downhill at 9.9 miles; use caution, as the road curves left, then right, on its way down. Turn right onto Highway 55 at 10.8 miles, followed by a left onto County EE at 11 miles.

Ride up to 11.3 miles for a beautiful view of Lake Winnebago, Wisconsin's largest inland lake spreading out before you; then turn left onto Lakeshore Drive at 11.4 miles. To get to Calumet County Park on the shore of Lake Winnebago, continue straight for a little more than a mile; just keep in mind that it will be all uphill getting back.

As you head down Lakeshore Drive, Lake Winnebago stays in view off to the right, with rolling farm fields to the left. Turn left onto Lake Street at 13.6 miles and continue into Stockbridge and a stop at Highway 55, at 14.3 miles. The ridge of the Niagara Escarpment can be clearly seen ahead.

Turn right onto Highway 55 and then a left onto Hickory Hills Road at 14.7 miles. You'll gradually work your way up onto the escarpment at 16.3 miles for some more good views of the lake and rolling countryside. At 17.1 miles turn right onto Long Road, which curves left and joins Shady Lane Road (which doesn't have much shade that I could see) to weave through some farm fields. Then turn right onto Finnegan Road.

The ride on the ridge is much flatter with only a small hill now and then. At 19.8 miles turn left onto County F, then right onto Trucker Road, at 20.3 miles. A left turn onto Quinney Road heads to a stop at Highway 151, at 23.2 miles. Turn left and come back to the park at 23.7 miles.

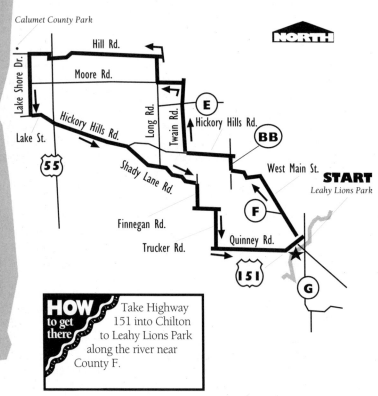

Calumet County Park

Hill Rd.

Lake Shore Dr.

Moore Rd.

Hickory Hills Rd.

Lake St.

**55**

Long Rd.

Twain Rd.

**E**

Hickory Hills Rd.

**BB**

West Main St.

**START**

*Leahy Lions Park*

Shady Lane Rd.

**F**

Finnegan Rd.

Trucker Rd.

Quinney Rd.

**151**

**G**

*Lake Winnebago*

**NORTH**

**HOW** to get there
Take Highway 151 into Chilton to Leahy Lions Park along the river near County F.

**DIRECTIONS at a glance**

0.0 From Leahy Lions Park turn right onto West Main Street.

0.1 Turn left onto South State Street (County F).

0.6 Continue straight on West Main Street as County F goes to the left.

2.8 Turn right onto County BB.

3.3 Turn left onto Hickory Hills Road.

4.5 Turn right onto Twain Road.

5.5 Cross County E.

6.2 Turn left onto Moore Road.

7.3 Turn right onto Long Road.

8.4 Turn left onto Hill Road.

10.8 Turn right onto Highway 55.

11.0 Turn left onto County EE.

11.4 Turn left onto Lake Shore Drive.

13.6 Turn left onto Lake Street.

14.3 Turn right onto Highway 55.

14.7 Turn left onto Hickory Hills Road.

17.1 Turn right onto Long Road.

17.6 Long Road curves left onto Shady Lane Road; continue on Shady Lane Road.

19.1 Turn right onto Finnegan Road.

19.8 Turn left onto County F.

20.3 Turn right onto Trucker Road.

21.8 Turn left onto Quinney Road.

23.2 Turn left onto Highway 151.

23.7 Return to park.

To find out more about the area, a good side trip by bike or car is to the Ledge View Nature Center. Head south from Chilton 2.5 miles on County G to a left turn onto Short Cut Road. The nature center is on top of the hill. The center sponsors an annual bike ride each year.

# A Tale of Two Rivers

| | |
|---:|:---|
| Number of miles: | 22.5 |
| Approximate pedaling time: | 2.5 hours |
| Terrain: | Slightly rolling |
| Traffic: | Light |
| Things to see: | Two Rivers, Rogers Street Historic Fishing Village, Berners Ice Cream Parlor, Nashota Park, Point Beach State Forest, East Twin River |
| Food: | Two Rivers; Steiners Corners at 13.2 miles; Corner Tavern at 16.8 miles |

Two Rivers is a holdover from the days when Lake Michigan was considered a major fishery and the economies of many of the shoreline communities depended on the bounty of this freshwater sea. The economy of Two Rivers is much more diverse these days, although it still depends heavily on commercial fishing, particularly through a thriving deepwater-charter industry. The Rogers Street Fishing Village on Jackson Street pays homage to Two Rivers' maritime past with a wide range of exhibits.

Of course, bicyclists might be more interested in the fact that Two Rivers claims to be the birthplace of the ice-cream sundae, created here in 1881 and sold then only on Sundays. Berners Ice Cream Parlor, operated by the Two Rivers Historical Society in the restored Washington House on Jefferson Street, will sell you an old-time sundae any day of the week.

Start this ride at Nashota Park. Park across 22nd Street/Highway 42 at the football field or in Nashota Park. It's a half mile down Pierce Street through the park to the beach on Lake Michigan. The ride begins on 22nd Street at Pierce Street, by the

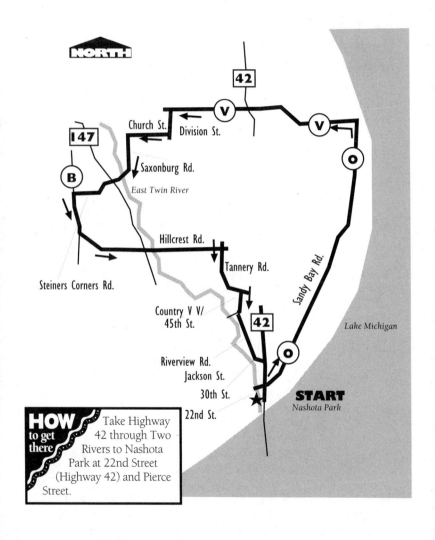

NORTH

42

Church St.
Division St.

147

Saxonburg Rd.

B

East Twin River

Hillcrest Rd.

Tannery Rd.

Steiners Corners Rd.

Country V V/
45th St.

42

Riverview Rd.
Jackson St.

O

30th St.

START
Nashota Park

22nd St.

V

V

O

Sandy Bay Rd.

Lake Michigan

HOW
to get
there
Take Highway
42 through Two
Rivers to Nashota
Park at 22nd Street
(Highway 42) and Pierce
Street.

**DIREC-TIONS at a glance**

| | | |
|---|---|---|
| 0.0 | From Nashota Park turn right onto 22nd Street |
| 0.1 | Continue straight onto Sandy Bay Road (County O). |
| 4.5 | Point Beach State Forest Headquarters. |
| 5.2 | Turn left onto County V. |
| 8.8 | Cross Highway 42. |
| 10.6 | Turn left onto Division Street. |
| 11.3 | Turn right onto Church Street. |
| 12.1 | Turn left onto Saxonburg Road. |
| 12.8 | Turn right onto Steiners Corners Road. |
| 13.2 | Cross Highway 147. |
| 14.3 | Turn left onto County B. |
| 15.1 | Turn left onto Hillcrest Road. |
| 18.4 | Turn right onto Tannery Road. |
| 19.7 | Turn right onto County VV (45th Street). |
| 20.1 | Turn left onto River View Road. |
| 21.3 | River View Road becomes 30th Street. |
| 21.4 | Turn right onto Jackson Street. |
| 22.1 | Turn left onto 22nd Street. |
| 22.5 | Return to Nashota Park. |

park sign. Turn onto 22nd Street and immediately continue straight onto Sandy Bay Road/County O. An officially designated Rustic Road, this will take you into Point Beach State Forest. Look to the right occasionally and you'll see sand dunes covered with scrub brush and pines.

After 3.3 miles there are no houses or other development, just a pleasant ride through dense forest. The Point Beach State Forest Headquarters are at 4.5 miles on the right. Turn in here and, in a half mile, you're on the beach with a view of Rawley Point Lighthouse; the waters off the point have claimed more than 30 vessels over the years. Continuing into the forest will take you to a concessions area, a campground, and a pristine beach.

Back on Sandy Bay Road, continue northeast, passing the campgrounds to your right at 5 miles on a gradual downhill. At 5.2 miles County O ends with a view of Lake Michigan through the trees. Follow the road to the left as it becomes County V. Climb up a gradual hill away from the lake. By 7 miles you're up into rural countryside. (For a side trip to the Point Beach Nuclear Power Plant, turn north onto Lakeshore Road for 3 miles.) Pass a wetland restoration project on the right at 7.5 miles; then ride into flat farmland. Cross Highway 42 at 8.8 miles and continue west on County V. At 10.6 miles turn left onto Division Drive, then right onto Church Street at 11.3 miles. Cross a creek and then ride up a slight hill to a left turn onto Saxonburg Road at 12.1 miles.

The road curves a little with the East Twin River—one of the two rivers, along with the West Twin, that give the city its name—to your right. On a slight downhill come to a Y and continue right (no stop) onto Steiners Corners Road. Cross the East Twin River and then stop at 13.2 miles, Highway 147, where you can find food and refreshment and two country inns.

Continue straight on a curving, flat rural road to a left turn onto County B at 14.3 miles, then a left on Hillcrest Road at 15.1 miles. Pass an unusual collection of weathered-wood buildings at 16 miles on the way to a stop at 16.8 miles to cross Highway 147. There's a tavern here for food or refreshments. Cross the river at 17 miles; then head up a steady climb to 18 miles. Turn right onto Tannery Road at 18.4 miles. Follow Tannery as it sweeps to the left, continue past Maplewood Road at 19 miles, and then turn right onto County VV/45th Street at 19.7 miles. At 20.1 miles turn left onto River View Road.

River View Road meanders back into Two Rivers, with the East Twin River to your right and the city ahead. Just before the stop at Jackson Street at 21.4 miles, River View Road becomes 30th Street. Turn right onto Jackson Street through a residential neighborhood to 22nd Street at 21.2 miles. Turn left onto 22nd Street and you'll be back at the park at 22.5 miles.

# North Kettles Cruise

Number of miles: 14.7
Approximate pedaling time: 1.5 hours
Terrain: Slightly to moderately rolling throughout
Traffic: Light
Things to see: Old Wade House State Park, Kettle Moraine State Forest, Parnell Tower
Food: Greenbush

Visiting Old Wade House State Park at Greenbush is like traveling in time to the nineteenth century. The park includes a number of restored buildings from the early 1800s, when Greenbush was an important stop on the plank road between Sheboygan and Fond du Lac. Included are a carriage museum, a blacksmith shop, and the Old Wade House itself, a restored stagecoach inn and halfway house built between 1847 and 1851. In 1860 the railroad bypassed Greenbush by 2 miles, and the once-prosperous village was frozen in time.

This ride starts at the historic marker next to the Old Wade House and travels through a portion of the Northern Unit of the Kettle Moraine State Forest. Ride south on Old Plank Road to a right turn onto County T. At eight-tenths of a mile, turn left onto Kettle Moraine Drive.

The glacier that covered Wisconsin 10,000 years ago left many defining features behind in this area. The deep cuplike depressions, kettles, are as common as the sharp, tree-covered ridges, the moraines, in this 28,000-acre forest that ranges for 25 miles south from Greenbush. Kettle Moraine Drive is a cyclist's delight as it twists and turns, drops down, and then bobs up

through the forest. There are hills, almost constant hills, but few long, strenuous climbs. Continue past Spring Valley Road on the right at 1.4 miles to one of the more challenging hills on the ride, a twisting climb through a dense forest to 1.8 miles. The Greenbush Recreation Area is on the right as the road goes down, then back up and around to the right at 2.4 miles. There are nice views on both sides of the road from this high point before a fast downhill at 2.9 miles. Be careful of your speed as the road corkscrews down, passing a kettle-bowl depression on the right at 3.3 miles.

Stay to the right on Kettle Moraine Drive at 3.4 miles, where Summit Road goes straight. The scenery opens up a bit here; a farm field to the left provides a view of the rolling moraines off in the distance. Turn right onto Highway 67 at 4.2 miles and then take the next right onto Forest Road at 4.6 miles through rolling farm country. Turn left onto County U at 5.4 miles and drop down a hill to a stop at Highway 67, 6 miles. Turn right onto Highway 67, then back onto County U at 6.3 to the left. County U goes left here, but continue straight onto Woodside Drive. Follow this downhill to a 90-degree left turn. Turn right back onto County U at 7.6 miles and follow it as it swings around to the left. The road begins with a gentle climb and then becomes steeper as you get to 8.6 miles. Pull in at Parnell Tower, about a half mile back from the road, for a climb to the top of the tower and a stunning view of the rolling countryside below.

Stop at County U/County A at 8.9 miles and turn left. At 9.5 miles County U goes right, but continue straight onto County A into a series of roller-coaster hills. Drop down at 9.9 miles and swing to the left for a great view, following a gradual downhill out of the woods at 10.4 miles into typical farm country.

Turn right onto Highway 67 at 10.8 miles, then left onto County A at 11 miles. Head up a hill that is at first deceptively gradual but quickly increases its grade to about 11.4 miles, leading into a number of short little hills. Swing to the right and pass County Z at 12.5 miles. Climb onto a ridge in the forest at 13 miles. From here enjoy a wonderful serpentine ride that

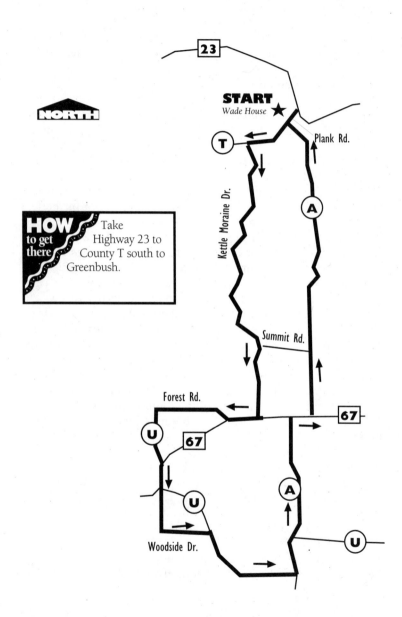

23

NORTH

START
Wade House

T

Plank Rd.

A

Kettle Moraine Dr.

HOW to get there Take Highway 23 to County T south to Greenbush.

Summit Rd.

Forest Rd.

67

U

67

U

A

U

Woodside Dr.

**DIREC-
TIONS
at a glance**

0.0 From the historic marker at the Old Wade House, go straight on Plank Road.
0.1 Turn right onto County T.
0.8 Turn left onto Kettle Moraine Drive.
3.4 Stay right on Kettle Moraine Drive (Summit Road goes straight).
4.2 Turn right onto Highway 67.
4.6 Turn right onto Forest Road.
5.4 Turn left onto County U.
6.0 Turn right onto Highway 67/County U.
6.3 Turn left onto County U.
6.4 Continue straight onto Woodside Drive.
7.6 Turn right onto County U.
8.9 Turn left onto County U/County A.
9.4 Continue straight onto County A (County U turns left).
10.8 Turn right onto Highway 67/County A.
11.0 Turn left onto County A.
14.4 Turn left onto County A/Plank Road.
14.7 Return to Old Wade House.

swings down into a hardwood forest, but keep your eyes open for gravel on some of the turns. Pop out into the open at 13.8 miles as the downhill fun continues.

At 14.4 miles turn left onto Plank Road/County A and return to the historic-marker starting point at 14.7 miles. If you haven't done it yet, visit the Old Wade House and the other buildings in the park. There's a visitor center and large parking lot a half mile behind the Old Wade House.

# Yachts of Fun at Green Lake

|                              |                                                                                              |
| ---------------------------: | -------------------------------------------------------------------------------------------- |
|           **Number of miles:** | 12.9                                                                                         |
|   **Approximate pedaling time:** | 1.5 hours                                                                                    |
|                    **Terrain:** | Flat near the lake; rolling, with a couple of moderate climbs, in the countryside            |
|                    **Traffic:** | Light                                                                                        |
|              **Things to see:** | Lake Geneva, lakeshore homes, Schwartz Gallery Park, Sunset Park, Lions Park                  |
|                       **Food:** | Lake Geneva                                                                                   |

The town of Green Lake is the oldest resort community in Wisconsin, often billed as the oldest resort community west of Niagara Falls. Portions of the lake are rimmed by stately homes, proof that there's also a lot of old money in Green Lake. Seven and a half miles long, 2 miles wide, and more than 230 feet deep, Green Lake is Wisconsin's deepest spring-fed lake.

Start from Lions Park on South Street/Business Highway 23 a half block from County A/Mill Street. Turn right out of the park, cross Mill Street to the next right, a block away, onto Lake Street, and ride through a residential area. Turn left at six-tenths of a mile onto Illinois Street and cruise past some opulent lakeshore mansions, several with garages bigger than many ordinary homes. Your mother might have told you it's not polite to stare, but you won't be able to help yourself as you pass by these homes. A golf course is on the left at 1 mile before a stop at County A, 1.8 miles.

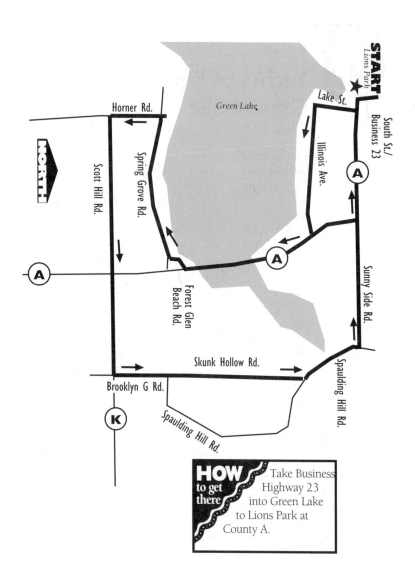

START
Lions Park

Green Lake

Horner Rd.

Lake St.

South St./
Business 23

NORTH

Scott Hill Rd.

Spring Grove Rd.

Illinois Ave.

A

A

A

Forest Glen Beach Rd.

Sunny Side Rd.

Skunk Hollow Rd.

Brooklyn G Rd.

K

Spaulding Hill Rd.

Spaulding Hill Rd.

**HOW to get there** Take Business Highway 23 into Green Lake to Lions Park at County A.

**DIREC-TIONS at a glance**

0.0 From Lions Park turn right onto South Street/Business Highway 23.
0.1 Turn right onto Lake Street.
0.6 Turn left onto Illinois Avenue.
1.8 Turn right onto County A.
3.2 Turn right onto Forest Glen Beach Road.
3.4 Turn right onto Spring Grove Road.
4.9 Turn left onto Horner Road.
5.4 Turn left onto Scott Hill Road.
6.9 Continue straight onto County K.
7.9 Turn left onto Brooklyn G Road.
8.4 Continue straight onto Skunk Hollow Road.
9.9 Turn left onto Spaulding Hill Road.
10.4 Turn left onto Sunnyside Road.
11.7 Cross County A.
12.9 Return to Lions Park.

Turn right onto County A and ride a wide paved shoulder toward the lake and Sunset Park, a public swimming beach, on the right. At 2.8 miles cross the eastern tip of the lake. Turn right onto Forest Glen Beach Road at 3.2 miles, then right on Spring Grove Road at 3.4 miles. Spring Grove is a narrow, winding road that rolls up and down along the southeastern shore of the lake through an area of smaller homes and cottages. There's an interesting log home on the left just after the turn onto Spring Grove.

A boat-dock area at 4.5 miles is a good place to stop, look out across the lake and watch the yachts and sailboats play on the water. Just past the boat dock is the massive fenced-and-guarded Sunrise Point Resort and Yacht Club (I wouldn't bother asking to use the bathroom here). At 4.9 miles turn left onto Horner Road and begin a climb up and away from the lake immediately into rural farm country, a striking contrast to the resort community below. Turn left onto Scott Hill Road at 5.4

miles and continue to climb. Although there's a lot of elevation gain coming away from the lake, the grades are not grinder-variety steep. By 6.1 miles you can look off to the left and see a rim of trees outlining Lake Geneva and get a sense of how far you've climbed. In a matter of a few miles, you've left behind the resort atmosphere for typical Wisconsin farmland.

Scott Hill Road takes you through a series of rolling hills to 6.9 miles and a stop at County A. Just before the stop look off to the left for an odd assortment of strange metal sculptures that cover the hillside. There's a visitor center just ahead to the left if you want to find out more about Schwartz Gallery Park.

Continue straight across County A onto County K, a wide, flat road. Turn left onto Brooklyn G Road at 7.9 miles to Skunk Hollow Road at 8.4 miles. Brooklyn G goes off to the right; continue straight on Skunk Hollow Road. Drop straight down Skunk Hollow Road for a quarter mile. This is a steep, exhilarating drop that will give you enough speed to coast halfway up the other side, before having to do it again over the next hill. There's a nice spot for looking out across to Green Lake at 9.8 miles, just before a left turn onto Spaulding Lake Road. Here there's another good view of the lake as the road swings down across a creek and through a wetland. At 10.4 miles come up to a left turn onto Sunnyside Road.

After cresting a small hill, Sunnyside Road drops down before climbing again to 11 miles, where you can see the water tower for Green Lake in the distance. Cross County A at 11.7 miles; then enjoy a nice downhill back into town. Cross Mill Street at 12.8 miles and you're back at the park at 12.9 miles.

Green Lake has a number of fine restaurants and an assortment of gift, antiques, and specialty shops. Check them out by riding or walking through the town.

# The Sites of Cedarburg

| | |
|---:|:---|
| **Number of miles:** | 12.3 |
| **Approximate pedaling time:** | 1.5 hours |
| **Terrain:** | Slightly rolling |
| **Traffic:** | Light to moderate in Grafton and Cedarburg |
| **Things to see:** | Arts and crafts shops in Cedarburg, Milwaukee River, Lake Michigan, Octagon Farms, Cedar Creek Park, Lime Kiln Park |
| **Food:** | Cedarburg |

Unlike many of the small towns that surround Greater Milwaukee, Cedarburg is not just a bedroom community of former urban dwellers seeking a quieter life, albeit with a long commute into the city. Cedarburg has a definite sense of itself and an identity all its own.

Downtown Cedarburg has been designated a National Historic District. Its distinctive limestone-and-brick buildings lend the city an air of Norman Rockwell civility. Cedarburg has a well-earned reputation for arts and crafts, brought about in large part by the Cedar Creek Settlement, a collection of about thirty shops, boutiques, and galleries that are housed in the restored 1864 Cedar Creek Woolen Mills complex on Bridge Street and Washington Avenue. There's also the Paul J. Yank's Brewery Works Fine Arts Complex, the Cedar Creek Winery, and a main street lined with unique shops. The Cedarburg Cultural Center on Washington Street puts it all into perspective, with changing exhibits on past and present Cedarburg.

The ride begins at Cedar Creek Park on Portland Road, along

the banks of Cedar Creek, two blocks from downtown. Park anywhere you can and start your mileage counter near the cascading waters of the creek near Portland and Columbia Streets. Head away from town on Portland, passing Legion Park on the right. There's a slight uphill on the way out of town, then a drop past a cluster of taverns as the road crosses Cedar Creek and becomes County T/Lakefield Road at eight-tenths of a mile. Climb up and away from the creek bed and continue past Green Bay Road at 1.2 miles. Climb a bit more into rural countryside and then enjoy a good downhill, crossing the Milwaukee River at 2 miles. Climb away from the river to a right turn onto County W at 3 miles.

County W has more traffic than County T, but it is flat with a paved shoulder. Turn left at the stoplights onto County C at 4 miles, cross over Highway 43, and then pass a large horse farm beginning at 4.5 miles. At 5 miles the road veers left—you have no choice but to follow it—and you see some large, elegant homes along the right. Lake Michigan is just behind the homes, although this is about as close to its shore as you'll get.

At about 5.5 miles the turn-of-the-century octagon barn on the right will catch your eye. This is Octagon Farms, where you can cruise in to see llamas, alpacas, and emus. Chances are you'll see them from the roadway if you don't want to make a stop.

At 6 miles turn right onto Lake Shore Drive for a few glimpses of Lake Michigan. Turn left onto Falls Road at 7.3 miles and head back toward Cedarburg. The road stays reasonably flat, but there is a bit of a gradual climb past County Q at 7.8 miles.

Cross Highway 43 and County W again and enjoy the ride down at 9.4 miles. Coming into the south end of Grafton, there's a sharp contrast between the spread of the town to the north and farm fields to the south. You're likely to see tractors compete with Saabs and Mercedes on these back roads, as new homes and condos spring up in what were once farm fields. Cross the Milwaukee River on a beautiful bridge at 9.8 miles and turn left onto Green Bay Road/Falls Road. Turn left again onto Green Bay Road at 10.2 miles, where Falls Road goes to the right.

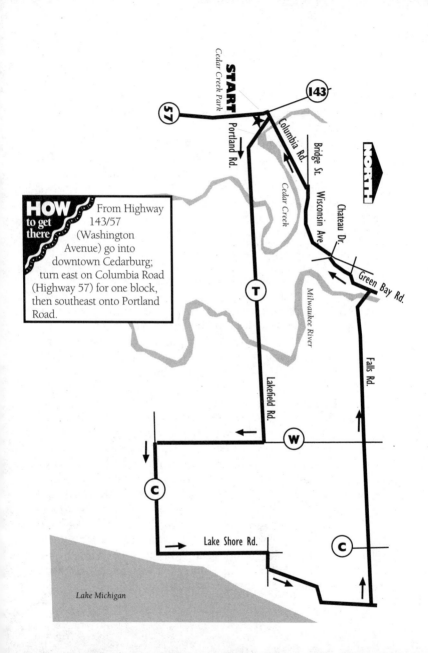

**START**

**57**

**143**

Cedar Creek Park

Portland Rd.

Columbia Rd.

Bridge St.

Wisconsin Ave.

Chateau Dr.

**NORTH**

Cedar Creek

Green Bay Rd.

**HOW**
to get
there
From Highway 143/57 (Washington Avenue) go into downtown Cedarburg; turn east on Columbia Road (Highway 57) for one block, then southeast onto Portland Road.

Milwaukee River

**T**

Falls Rd.

Lakefield Rd.

**W**

**C**

Lake Shore Rd.

**C**

Lake Michigan

**DIREC-TIONS at a glance**

| 0.0 | From Cedar Creek Park take Portland Road, heading away from the downtown area. |
|---|---|
| 0.4 | Portland Road becomes Lakefield Road/County T. |
| 3.0 | Turn right onto County W. |
| 4.0 | Turn left onto County C. |
| 6.0 | Turn left onto Lake Shore Road. |
| 7.3 | Turn left onto Falls Road. |
| 7.8 | Continue straight past County C. |
| 8.8 | Continue straight past County W. |
| 10.2 | Turn left onto Green Bay Road/Falls Road. |
| 10.4 | Turn left onto Green Bay Road. |
| 10.8 | Take next right turn onto Chateau Drive (no sign). |
| 10.9 | Turn left onto Wisconsin Avenue/Highway 57. |
| 11.6 | Continue straight onto Columbia Road. |
| 12.2 | Turn left onto Portland Road. |
| 12.3 | Return to park. |

Lime Kiln Park is on the left, with the old kilns for firing bricks still standing. At 10.8 miles stop, then turn right onto Chateau Drive. There's no street sign here; just be sure to take the next right after the park. Cross the railroad tracks and turn left onto Wisconsin Avenue/Highway 57.

Highway 57 is wide (four lanes) here as it angles back into Cedarburg, then narrows to a typical residential city street. At the stoplights at 11.6 miles, stay a bit to the left onto Columbia Road, not right onto Bridge Street—unless you want to go directly to Cedar Creek Settlement, which is at the intersection of Bridge Street and Washington Avenue. Turning onto Columbia Road, however, leads back to downtown Cedarburg. A block before Washington Avenue, turn left onto Portland Road and you're back at the starting point at 12.3 miles.

# Pike Lake and Those Holy Hills

| | |
|---:|:---|
| Number of miles: | 19.4 |
| Approximate pedaling time: | 2 hours |
| Terrain: | Rolling throughout |
| Traffic: | Light |
| Things to see: | Pike Lake, Holy Hill, Friess Lake |
| Food: | Water at Pike Lake State Park; Holy Hill at 6.8 miles; Fox and Hounds at 12.3 miles; Taverns at 7.9 and 13.8 miles |

There are a number of stories surrounding the Carmelite Monastery at Holy Hill. One legend has it that, in the mid-1800s, a local resident erected a huge cross on a ridge at the current site of the monastery. A French hermit who worshipped at the cross experienced a miraculous cure, and pilgrims have flocked to the site ever since. I like the somewhat similar story of François Soubris, a Quebec monk who had read Father Marquette's diary of his journey through Wisconsin in 1673. Marquette is said to have erected a cross on the hill and dedicated the site as holy ground. Seeking absolution for a less-than-holy life, Soubris went to Holy Hill to pray. Struck by a serious illness on his way to the site, Soubris climbed the hill on hands and knees and prayed for recovery. In the morning he was cured. After riding 20 miles through this countryside, you, too, might be praying for a cure when you're done.

Although the ride is hilly, there are few giant climbs. You'll use your lowest gears frequently, but there's as much down—and

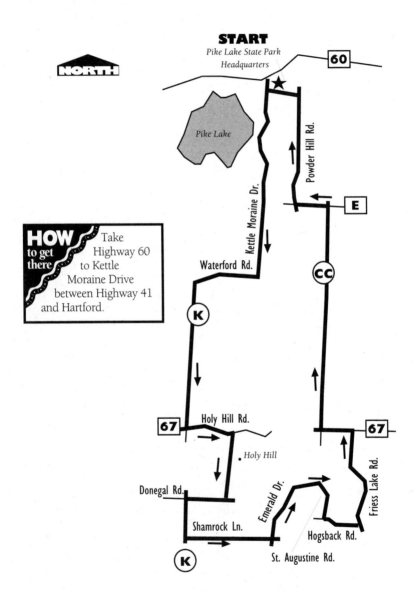

**DIREC-TIONS at a glance**

| | |
|---|---|
| 0.0 | From Pike Lake State Park, turn left onto Kettle Moraine Drive. |
| 1.6 | Cross County E. |
| 2.6 | Turn right onto Waterford Road. |
| 3.7 | Turn left onto County K. |
| 5.7 | Turn left onto Highway 67/Holy Hill Road. |
| 6.3 | Turn right into Holy Hill. |
| 6.8 | Continue past parking area down exit road. |
| 7.4 | Turn right onto Donegal Road. |
| 7.9 | Turn left onto County K. |
| 8.4 | Turn left onto Shamrock Lane. |
| 9.6 | Turn left onto Emerald Drive as Shamrock Lane ends. |
| 10.8 | Turn right onto St. Augustine Road. |
| 11.2 | Stay left (Hogsback Road; no sign) as St. Augustine goes right. |
| 11.9 | Turn left onto Friess Lake Road. |
| 13.3 | Turn left onto Highway 67. |
| 13.8 | Turn right onto County CC. |
| 16.8 | Turn left onto County E. |
| 17.3 | Turn right onto Powder Hill Road. |
| 18.8 | Turn left into Pike Lake State Park. |
| 19.4 | Return to parking lot. |

some of it spectacular—as there is up. And the scenery puts this ride in anyone's top ten. Take your time and enjoy every mile, even those that go up.

Begin at Pike Lake State Park, which spans both sides of Kettle Moraine Drive south of Highway 60. The lake is west of the road, and camping facilities and trails are on the bluffs to the east. From the parking lot at park headquarters, turn left onto Kettle Moraine Drive and begin the pattern of up-and-down riding that will continue throughout the ride.

At the top of the first hill, look out to the right onto Pike Lake. After another up and down, pass by the lake at seven-tenths of a mile, where there's a beach and picnic area. Go up and down again before crossing County E at 1.6 miles to see the next hill you have to climb up ahead. Drop down at 2 miles, ride up for a half mile, and then enjoy a nice downhill. Ride the brakes, however, because you'll turn right at 2.6 miles onto Waterford Road.

More rolling hills lead to a swing to the right on a tight downhill to County K at 3.7 miles. Turn left, then head up and down again, catching a glimpse of the spires of Holy Hill to the left, and climb from 4.9 miles to 5.5 miles. Turn left at 5.7 miles onto Highway 167/Holy Hill Road. A nice forested road leads up to the entrance of Holy Hill at 6.3 miles on the right. Ride up here to the parking lot at 6.8 miles, and you'll be at the base of the Holy Hill National Shrine of Mary. Take a break and walk up the winding staircase into the spires for an incredible view of the surrounding countryside.

Head down the exit road to the north, a great downhill run through a dense forest, to a right turn onto Donegal Road at 7.4 miles. Follow Donegal Road to County K at 7.9 miles. The Erin Tavern across the road has food and beverages.

Turn left onto County K, then left again, at 8.4 miles, onto Shamrock Road, an officially designated Rustic Road. Start on a flat and then have fun on a short, quarter-mile downhill before climbing from 9.2 miles to a left onto Emerald Drive at 9.6 miles. The next 3.5 miles are about the prettiest you'll find anywhere.

Climb a little hill onto a ridge and look out to Holy Hill at 9.9 miles on the distant ridge to the left. Passing Donegal Road at 10.2 miles, ride through a tunnel of trees and look for the houses, tucked into the hillsides, that blend into their surroundings. The road twists and turns, rolling up and down before a right turn onto St. Augustine Road at 10.8 miles. Drop down and swing to the left. St. Augustine Road goes to the right, but stay left; this is Hogsback Road, although there is no sign to help you. Just be sure to stay left. The views here are spectacular, with valleys on both sides as you ride a sharp ridge. Turn left onto Friess Lake Road at 11.9 miles for still more serpentine riding along a tree-lined road. The popular Fox and Hounds Restaurant is on the right at 12.3 miles, and you'll pass Glacial Hills County Park at 13 miles.

Turn left onto Highway 167 at 13.3 miles, climb to a right onto County CC—there's a pub here if you need refreshments—and continue through rolling hills and farm fields to a left turn onto County E at 16.8 miles. Go up slightly, and when you see ponds on both sides of the road, get ready to turn right onto Powder Hill Road at 17.3 miles.

Ride up for a half mile before the road flattens out a bit; then roll through some more hills to a left turn at 18.8 miles back into the park. Turn at the sign that says BEACH, PICNIC, OFFICE. It's pretty much all downhill from here back to the parking lot at 19.4 miles.

# Milwaukee: Mansions, Lake Michigan, and the 76 Trail

| | |
|---|---|
| **Number of miles:** | 11.2 miles |
| **Approximate pedaling time:** | 1.5 hours |
| **Terrain:** | Flat, with a few slight hills |
| **Traffic:** | Light to moderate |
| **Things to see:** | Lake Michigan, parkways, bike trail, and mansions |
| **Food:** | Throughout the ride |

To outsiders Milwaukee has a not-unfounded blue-collar reputation as a city of bratwurst, bowling, and beer; yet Milwaukee is much more than all that. It's a lively city of festivals and parks, arts and entertainment. Decaying downtown areas are being rejuvenated, old neighborhoods are being restored, and new, smaller industries are replacing the large, outdated manufacturing plants that have closed or moved away. The beer that made Milwaukee famous, as the ads once proclaimed, has long left the city; in fact, "Beer City" is down to just one major brewery. Milwaukee is a changing city, and though it might not be appreciated nationwide, it's not surprising to Milwaukeeans that, in 1996, *Fortune* magazine called their town one of the most livable cities in the country.

This is a short, easy ride that barely touches on what Milwaukee has to offer yet still calls attention to some of the city's charms. Begin at the far parking lot, the one nearest the lake, on Lagoon Drive at Veterans Park, just off Lincoln Memorial Drive. If the lot is full (and there's a good chance of that in summer),

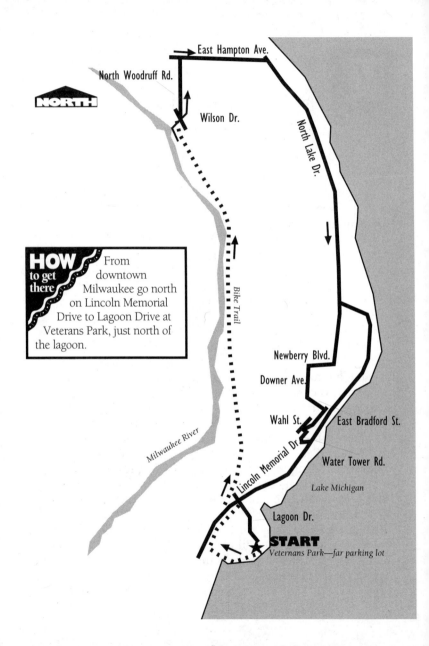

NORTH

East Hampton Ave.

North Woodruff Rd.

Wilson Dr.

North Lake Dr.

**HOW** to get there — From downtown Milwaukee go north on Lincoln Memorial Drive to Lagoon Drive at Veterans Park, just north of the lagoon.

Bike Trail

Milwaukee River

Newberry Blvd.

Downer Ave.

Wahl St.

East Bradford St.

Lincoln Memorial Dr.

Water Tower Rd.

Lake Michigan

Lagoon Dr.

**START**
Veternans Park—far parking lot

**DIREC-TIONS at a glance**

0.0 From the far parking lot at Veterans Park, pedal directly toward Lake Michigan; turn right onto the bike path.

0.5 Follow path to the right toward Lincoln Memorial Drive.

0.7 Follow path between lagoon and Lincoln Memorial Drive.

1.2 At Lagoon Drive cross to continuation of bike path.

4.9 Turn left onto North Woodruff Avenue.

5.3 Turn right onto East Hampton Avenue.

6.0 Turn right onto North Lake Drive.

8.5 Turn right onto Newberry Boulevard.

8.8 Turn left onto Downer Avenue.

9.2 Turn left onto East Bradford Street.

9.4 Turn right onto Wahl Street.

9.6 Turn left onto Water Tower Road.

9.9 Turn right onto Lincoln Memorial Drive.

10.7 Turn left onto Lagoon Drive.

11.2 Return to parking lot.

park along the park road or in another lot and ride up to the far lot to begin your mileage counter.

Head straight toward Lake Michigan, past the concessions stand and the bathrooms, to a right turn down the path along the lakefront. The building on the hill ahead is the War Memorial, which also houses the Milwaukee Art Museum. As you leave the water's edge, follow the path that heads toward Lincoln Memorial Drive and angles toward the right; don't take the 90-degree right. Stay on the path as it passes between Lincoln Memorial Drive and the lagoon and then leads back to Lagoon Drive at 1.2 miles. Cross Lincoln Memorial Drive here and head right on the bike path.

This paved path is a small segment of a much larger bikeway system, the 76 Trail, that completely circles the Greater Milwaukee area; it would take you a day to ride the entire trail. The path here follows an abandoned railroad right-of-way through the city to the northern suburbs; when you get off in a few miles, you'll be in a different kind of world entirely. With high banks on both sides, the ride along here is completely isolated from the city you're passing through. Pass the exit at Cambridge Woods, at 3.5 miles, which will take you to the University of Wisconsin–Milwaukee. Cross over Capitol Drive at 4.1 miles, pass Eastabrook Park on the left, at 4.3 miles, and then exit the trail where the pavement ends, at 4.7 miles.

Cross over Wilson Drive and take the first left onto North Woodruff Avenue into the quiet neighborhood of Shorewood. Four blocks later, after cresting a small hill, turn right onto East Hampton Avenue, at 5.3 miles in Whitefish Bay. Continue east on Hampton, riding up and over a small hill, to a right turn onto North Lake Drive, at 6 miles.

North Lake Drive is fairly wide, with moderate traffic, but it is a street used often by bicyclists. Although the residents might feel slightly uncomfortable, take your time checking out the scenery as you roll along past some of the more elegant homes in the Milwaukee area. You'll catch glimpses of the sprawling mansions, often behind gated and brick-walled fences, on the bluff above Lake Michigan. Shorewood Park at Capitol Drive, 7.1 miles, is a nice place to stop and look out over the lake.

Pass East Kenwood Boulevard at 8.3 miles—a left turn here will take you along the lakefront—and continue straight, with Lake Park on the left. Turn right onto Newberry Boulevard, a true divided street boulevard, at 8.5 miles. A side trip down any of the streets off Newberry is rewarded with more elegant old homes; check out the one on the corner of Summit and Newberry.

Turn left onto Downer Avenue at 8.8 miles and cruise through a little neighborhood of bistros, unique shops, food stores, and restaurants. Go through the stoplights at East Belleview Street to the next left turn, at 9.2 miles, onto East Bradford Street and head back toward the lake. Cross North Lake Drive; then turn right onto Wahl Avenue at 9.4 miles. The parkway along the bluff to your left overlooks the lake.

Stop at Terrace Avenue and then continue left down Water Tower Road at 9.6 miles. The old brick water tower in front of St. Mary's Hospital was a popular hippie gathering spot in the 1960s. Hang onto your brakes as you wind down Water Tower Road and come back to Lincoln Memorial Drive at 9.9 miles. A left takes you along Bradford Beach toward Lake Park. Turn right to head back to Veterans Park.

Paths line both sides of Lincoln Memorial Drive and will likely be full of other cyclists, strollers, runners, and inline skaters. Swing into McKinley Marina to check out some of the large pleasure boats that ply these waters, or just ride slowly along the path, enjoying the scenery. Continue past the stoplights at Lafayette Hill Road and turn back into Veterans Park on Lagoon Drive, at 10.7 miles. The far parking lot is at 11.2 miles.

# Tour de Fort

| | |
|---:|:---|
| **Number of miles:** | 20.3 |
| **Approximate pedaling time:** | 2.5 hours |
| **Terrain:** | Flat to gently rolling, with an occasional steep climb |
| **Traffic:** | Light in the country; moderate through Fort Atkinson |
| **Things to see:** | Towns of Fort Atkinson and Cold Spring, Hoard Historical Museum and Dairy Shrine, Fireside Restaurant and Playhouse, Glacial Lake Trail, Lake Koshkonong, Rock and Bark Rivers |

If Wisconsin is "America's Dairyland," then Fort Atkinson can be considered Wisconsin's hometown. Former Governor W. D. Hoard of Fort Atkinson is considered to be the father of the state's dairy industry, and his 1860s era mansion is now a shrine to that industry. The Hoard Historical Museum and Dairy Shrine is just south of the Rock River on Highway 12.

The museum (and shrine) pays homage to the history of dairy farming in the United States through exhibits and a multimedia presentation. The museum also documents Wisconsin's most famous conflict between settlers and Native Americans, the Black Hawk War of 1832, and provides a history of the early Native Americans of the area. The Hoard grounds contain the restored 1841 pioneer home of Dwight Foster, the founder of Fort Atkinson.

History aside, Fort Atkinson is widely recognized for having one of the finest dinner theaters in the Midwest, the Fireside

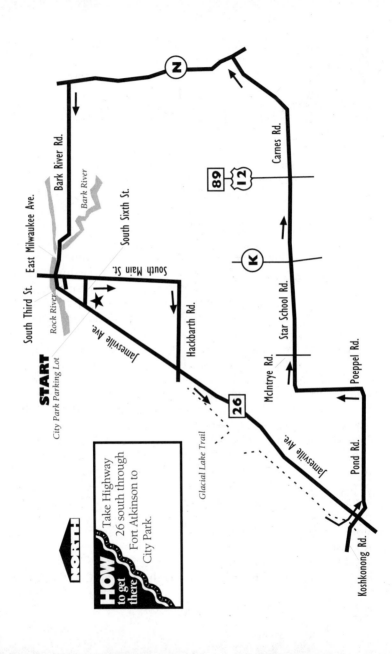

**DIRECTIONS at a glance**

0.0 From parking lot of City Park, turn right onto Janesville Avenue (Highway 26).

0.2 Turn right onto South Sixth Street.

0.5 Turn right onto South Main Street.

1.8 Turn right onto Hackbarth Road.

2.6 Cross Janesville Avenue (Highway 26) to Farmco Lane.

2.9 Begin Glacial Lake Trail.

3.9 Turn right, following trail signs onto roadway.

5.2 Follow signs from roadway back onto trail.

5.8 Turn right, following trail signs onto roadway.

6.0 Turn left onto trail.

7.5 Trail ends. Turn left onto Koshkonong Road.

7.6 Cross Highway 26 to Pond Road.

8.6 Continue straight onto Poeppel Road.

10.2 At intersection with McIntyre Road, continue straight onto Star School Road.

11.4 Cross County K.

12.1 Cross Highway 12/89. Star School Road ends; Carnes Road begins. Continue straight on Carnes Road.

14.4 Turn left onto County N.

16.7 Turn left onto Bark River Road.

18.8 Turn left onto Bark River Road (becomes East Milwaukee Avenue).

19.6 Turn left onto South Main Street for one block.

19.7 Turn right onto South Third Street for one block.

19.9 Turn left onto Janesville Avenue.

20.3 Return to City Park parking lot.

Restaurant and Playhouse, just south of the Hoard Historical Museum. Finish your ride with dinner and what's guaranteed to be an enjoyable evening's live entertainment.

This ride pays homage to the Hoard heritage, as the road

passes through some of the picturesque farmland that made this region famous. Not as hilly as the country to the north and east, there are still a few climbs that will have you dropping into your lowest gears. As you leave the parking lot of the City Park, turn right onto Janesville Avenue for one block, passing the ball field; then turn right onto Sixth Street. Go two blocks, stop at and cross Grove Street, go two more blocks to cross Grant Street, and then go one block to a right turn onto South Main Street at five-tenths of a mile (all through a quiet residential neighborhood). Continue past Rockwell Avenue at eight-tenths of a mile for a short but steady climb.

Stop at Hackbarth Road, 1.8 miles, and turn right. There will be a bit of a climb, with the edge of the city to your right and farm fields to the left. Pass the water tower at 2.3 miles and then ride downhill to a stop at Janesville Avenue (Highway 26) at 2.6 miles. Cross Janesville to Farmco Lane, just to the right. The parking lot for the Glacial Lake Trail is at end of Farmco at 2.9 miles.

This new 4.2-mile trail is unusual for Wisconsin in that three-quarters of it is paved. Not particularly scenic (the trail runs close to Highway 26), it's a pleasant enough alternative to riding on the busy highway. Cross a wooden bridge a half mile down the trail and follow along to 3.9 miles, where the trail is interrupted. Follow the bike-trail signs to the right, onto the roadway, and to the left at 4.6 miles. Stay on the roadway as it passes beneath the highway and back onto the trail at 5.2 miles. The paved portion of the trail soon ends, giving way to a firm, crushed-limestone surface as you pass open fields on the right and Highway 26 close by (although somewhat obscured by trees and scrub brush) on the left. The trail ends at 7.5 miles, Koshkonong Road; Koshkonong Lake is just a mile to the right.

Turn left here and cross Highway 26 for Pond Road, just to the right across the highway (I flushed a blue heron from the pond as I passed by here late one summer). Enjoy a downhill to start but be ready for a steady quarter-mile grind up to 8.5 miles.

Continue straight from Pond Road onto Poeppel Road at 8.6

miles; then make an almost immediate 90-degree turn to the left, with more of a steady uphill. At 9.1 miles continue past Groeler Road, which comes in from the left, and then make another 90-degree turn, this time to the right. You'll soon enjoy a nice rolling downhill. Stop at the intersection with McIntyre Road, at 10.2 miles, and continue straight onto Star School Road. The ride flattens out a bit and then moves into a nice downhill at 10.8 miles. Stop at 11.4 miles to cross County K and continue along a gently rolling road through farm fields. Stop at Highway 12/89, at 12.1 miles, and continue straight to Carnes Road, just slightly to the left.

Carnes Road rolls through the farmland countryside after an S turn. As it bends to the northeast, it passes a quiet hillside cemetery at 14.1 miles and comes to an end at County N at 14.4 miles, at the small village of Cold Spring. The Cold Spring Inn can provide refreshments as well as a great meal.

Continue north on County N, passing County M at 15.4 miles, to a left turn onto Bark River Road at 16.7 miles. There will be a gradual downhill, then a gradual uphill past Kutz Road on the right at 17.9 miles. Just after Kutz Road stop at the freshwater well on the right side of the road at 18.1 miles. Drink from the spring and fill your water bottle; it's hard to explain, but the water has a distinct, nonfiltered, refreshing taste.

The ride is almost over, but the best part is yet to come. Just after you pass the well, you'll enter a river forest reminiscent of bayou country—a thick overhang of trees, the Bark River to the left, and a dense forest floor. Stop at 18.8 miles and turn left onto Bark River Road, which will become East Milwaukee Road as you come back into Fort Atkinson.

Now there are rivers on both sides of the road: the Bark on the left and the Rock on the right. Cross the bridge at 19 miles, where Bark River enters Rock River, and continue on to a left turn onto South Main Street at 19.6 miles. Back in the city now, go one block on South Main Street; then turn right at the lights onto South Third Street. Stop at Janesville Avenue at 19.9 miles and turn left. You're back at the parking lot at 20.3 miles.

Before you leave you might want to check out the Café Carpe on South Water Street, the informal headquarters for the Tour de Fort Bike Club and the "cultural" center (so club members say) for the city. The club stages an annual bike ride, the Tour de Fort, along this, and other, routes in the area.

# Chocolate City Delight

| | |
|---:|:---|
| **Number of miles:** | 24.5 |
| **Approximate pedaling time:** | 2 hours |
| **Terrain:** | Flat to slightly rolling, first half; some moderate hills, second half |
| **Traffic:** | Light except moderate in Burlington |
| **Things to see:** | Burlington, Echo Lake, Honey Lake, Honey Creek Wildlife Area, Rochester, Fox River, two Rustic Roads |
| **Food:** | Burlington, Honey Lake, Rochester, Highway 11 at 17.7 miles |

The name of this ride doesn't refer to an ice-cream sundae that originated in this southeastern Wisconsin city but to the city's largest employer, the Nestlé Company. If you're a chocolate lover and the wind is right, your mouth will be watering as you ride into or out of Burlington; at times the smell of rich, sweet chocolate hangs over the town. Keep that in mind, as a frozen-custard stand happens to be at the corner where the ride ends. It's almost impossible to resist a chocolate-covered treat when this ride is over. If you happen to do this ride in May, the Chocolate Festival—a large community-wide celebration with chocolate as the theme—might satisfy your craving for both the sweet stuff and a pleasant bike ride.

There is more to Burlington, however, than chocolate. The Spinning Top Exploratory Museum on Milwaukee Street features more than 2,000 yo-yos and gyroscopes as well as modern and antique tops. If you're in a contemplative mood, there's no better place than the gardens and grotto of the St. Francis Retreat Center, which you'll pass midway through the ride.

This is a pleasant ride, and you can trust me on that. (Even though Burlington is home to a nationally known Liars Club—the best fabrication is announced each year on New Year's Day—I am not a member.) Leave Echo Lake Veterans Memorial Park to the right and turn right at the stoplights, following the Highway 11 signs, onto Commerce Street. Continue on Highway 11 as it turns left onto Kendall Street at four-tenths of a mile and then take the next right onto Chestnut Street. Ride through a residential area, staying close to Echo Lake and passing Wagner Park on the right. At 1 mile turn right onto Bieneman Road, which crosses the west end of the lake and follows along Honey Creek. There's an interesting bridge that crosses the creek at 1.5 miles.

Turn left onto Spring Prairie Road at 1.9 miles and enter some farm country. Take the next road to the right, County DD at 3.4 miles, although there isn't a sign at the intersection. There are no steep hills in this half of the ride, but you will head gradually up, and by 4 miles you'll be up high enough to see the surrounding hills of the countryside partitioned by the irregular design of farm fields. A gentle downhill leads into the small town of Honey Creek on Honey Lake.

Pass through town, with the lake nearby to the right, and follow County DD to the left at 5.3 miles. At 5.7 miles turn right onto Oak Knoll Road, the first of two officially designated Rustic Roads on this ride. A gradual uphill to a nice view levels off, passing the Honey Creek Wildlife Area to the right at 7.5 miles. Turn right on Washington Avenue at 8.2 miles and then take the next right onto Heritage Road, another Rustic Road.

Heritage Road twists and turns through a rural residential area, crests a hill, and then comes down to a left turn onto County FF at 9.4 miles. Come into Rochester on the Fox River at 10.8 miles after a gentle, curving downhill and turn right onto County W/South Front Street at 11.2 miles. Rochester has a waterfront restaurant and some gift and antiques shops.

Face your first significant uphill on the way out of Rochester before passing the St. Francis Retreat Center on the right at 12.1

miles. Cross Highway 36/83 at 13.3 miles, cross the Fox River, and continue past County A at 13.7 miles. Turn left onto Ketterhagen Road at 14 miles.

The rest of the ride has more hills but nothing too strenuous. There's a lovely view from the top of the hill at 14.4 miles, a good drop at 15 miles, then a climb to 15.8 miles. Turn right onto English Settlement Road/County J at 16.7 miles and enjoy a flat, straight stretch through farm country. Cross Highway 11 at 17.7 miles (a small tavern here can take care of your refreshment needs) and head toward Mount Tom, that forested hill in the distance. Halfway up the hill turn right onto Mount Tom Road, at 19.1 miles, and climb to 19.4 miles to a ridge of rolling hills with a wonderful vista to the south.

Mount Tom Road squiggles along to a right turn onto Bushnell Road at 22 miles. Follow Bushnell back into town; if the wind is right, you'll be greeted by the wafting odor of sweet chocolate. At 23.7 miles pass the Burlington sign, cross State Street on Main Street at 24 miles, and follow the Highway 11 West signs. Turn left at the next street, Jefferson, cross the Fox River, and turn right onto Bridge Street at 24.2 miles. Take the next right onto Chestnut Street, 24.4 miles, cross another bridge and head for the stoplights. Adrian's Frozen Custard is on the corner, and the Echo Lake Park parking lot is just across the lights to the left, at 24.5 miles.

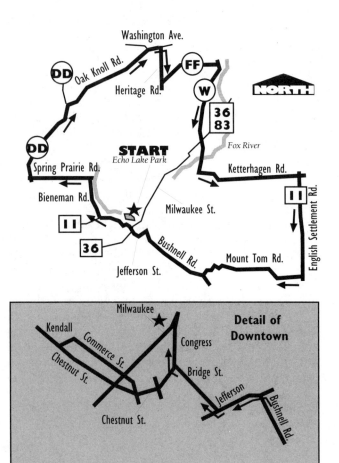

START
Echo Lake Park

**Detail of Downtown**

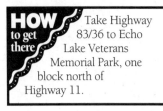

**HOW** to get there  Take Highway 83/36 to Echo Lake Veterans Memorial Park, one block north of Highway 11.

**DIREC-TIONS at a glance**

0.0   Exit right from the parking lot of Echo Lake Veterans Memorial Park.

0.1   At the next street, turn right onto Highway 11/Commerce Street.

0.4   Follow Highway 11 left onto Kendall Street; then make an immediate right turn onto Chestnut Street.

1.0   Turn right onto Bieneman Road.

1.9   Turn left onto Spring Prairie Road.

3.4   Turn right onto County DD.

5.3   Turn left, continuing on County DD.

5.7   Turn right onto Oak Knoll Road.

8.2   Turn right onto Washington Avenue.

8.5   Turn right onto Heritage Road.

9.4   Turn left onto County FF.

11.2   Turn right onto County W/South Front Street.

13.3   Cross Highway 36/83.

14.0   Turn left onto Ketterhagen Road.

16.7   Turn right onto English Settlement Road/County J.

17.7   Cross Highway 11.

19.1   Turn right onto Mount Tom Road.

22.0   Turn right onto Bushnell Road.

24.0   Bushnell becomes State Street once in the city limits. Cross State Street onto Main Street/Highway 11.

24.1   Following Highway 11, turn left onto Jefferson Street.

24.2   Turn right onto Bridge Street.

24.4   Turn right onto Chestnut Street.

24.5   Turn left onto Milwaukee Street; immediately after the left turn, turn right to return to the parking lot.

**Roun'da Manure and More**

| | |
|---:|:---|
| Number of miles: | 29.2 |
| Approximate pedaling time: | 3 hours |
| Terrain: | Flat to gently rolling, with one tough climb out of Fontana |
| Traffic: | Light in the country; moderate through towns |
| Things to see: | Towns of Fontana, Sharon, Darien, and Walworth; Lake Geneva; scenic countryside |
| Food: | At Fontana, Walworth, Sharon, Darien, Lake Delavan |

Sharon, a quaint town a mile north of the Wisconsin-Illinois border, is actually something of a bicycling mecca. Each summer Sharon hosts the Roun'da Manure bike ride, at one time touted by *Bicycling* magazine as one of the ten best rides in the country. (Roun'da Manure is a play on a French biking-related term as well as recognition of the Sharon area's many farms.) Besides the charms of Sharon, the ride appeals to families and beginning riders for its relatively gentle terrain and for the coupons you get to use at the many ice-cream shops in the area. This ride includes a bit of the Roun'da Manure route, as well as a connection to Lake Geneva.

Lake Geneva is Wisconsin's oldest resort destination. Before settlers had even made their first tentative forays into the northern wilds of the state, the well-to-do (many from the Chicago area less than 100 miles to the southeast) were making pilgrimages to the shores of Lake Geneva. The Wrigleys (yes, *those* Wrigleys) have an estate on the lake. There's still a feeling of prosperity, conspicuous consumption, and old money in the area, but that doesn't mean you can't have fun even if you're a budget bicyclist.

This ride starts at the far west end of Lake Geneva, in the small town of Fontana. Parking might be a bit of problem in the height of the summer season, although there are parking lots along the lakefront and along Fontana Boulevard. The ride starts from the lot in front of the gazebo at Reed Park.

Turn right out of the park; then turn left and head out Fontana Boulevard to Valley View Road (Highway 67). Turn left here and then take the next right, four-tenths of a mile, onto Dewey Road. From here you have a short but tough climb up and away from the lake. Gear down and head up, keeping in mind that the rest of the ride is gently rolling and basically flat and that you get to come *down* this same hill 29 miles from now.

At 1.6 miles turn left onto Townline Road and come rolling down into Walworth. At the town square you'll have to turn right, then left, around the square before a right turn out of town on Beloit Street at 2.6 miles. Relax now for a comfortable cruise into rural Wisconsin countryside.

Have you ever felt like trying sky diving? Here's your chance; pull into Stateline Sky Diving on the left at 5.2 miles. There's a good chance you might see some sky divers coming back to earth as you pass by. Cross County K at 6.6 miles and then begin a gradual uphill for the next half mile. At 8.7 miles turn left onto Bollinger Road for a gradual climb to 9.3 miles. At Highway 67, 10 miles, turn right onto County C. For food, water, and amenities, turn left and go a half mile into Sharon. To follow the route, turn right here.

Head north on County C on a flat, straight road past farm fields. Check out the earth-shelter home on the right, at 14.6 miles, and the interesting two-story brick home with a cupola at 15.4 miles. Turn right on County X at 16.1 miles for a gradual uphill into Darien.

Now might be a good time for an ice-cream break, and there just happens to be an ice-cream shop right at the intersection of

County X and Highway 14 in Darien at 17.2 miles. After the break continue on County X uphill and out of town. Turn right onto County K at 19 miles, where the countryside is a bit more rolling than in the Sharon area. Turn left onto Sweet Road at 20 miles, then right onto Elm Ridge Road at 20.9 miles, which gently rolls through farm country.

Turn left onto S&D Townline Road at 21.9 miles and head toward the southwest end of Delavan Lake. Cross County O at 22.6 miles, where there are restaurants and small inns for a refreshment break. The lake can be seen off to the left. Turn right onto Ox Lane Road just before Brown's Grocery at 23.8 miles, heading away from the lake through a pleasant rolling area. At 24.5 miles turn left onto North Walworth Road, then right onto Six Corners Road at 24.8 miles. There's a bit of a hill here that breaks into some rolling terrain, with a Christmas-tree plantation on the right and a huge dairy farm on the left.

Stop at Highway 14 at 26.8 miles and take the 90-degree left turn onto Brick Church Road immediately before Highway 14. There will be a climb here, gradual and long but not steep, then some roller-coaster ups and downs as you head back toward Fontana. As you approach the town, Brick Church Road becomes Dewey Road. Stop at Townline Road and then enjoy the hill you labored up to start the ride. Turn left onto Valley View Road (Highway 67), then right at 28.9 miles back onto Fontana Boulevard. At 29.2 miles you're back at the parking lot.

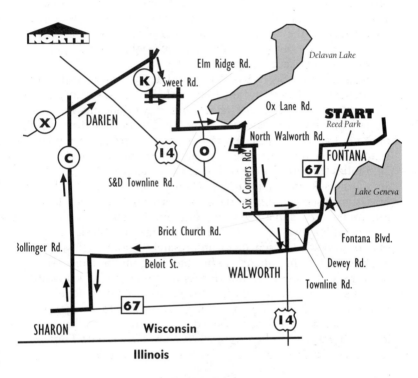

**NORTH**

Delavan Lake

Elm Ridge Rd.

**K** Sweet Rd.

Ox Lane Rd.

**START**
*Reed Park*

**X**

**DARIEN**

North Walworth Rd.

**FONTANA**

**C**

**14**

**O**

Six Corners Rd.

**67**

S&D Townline Rd.

Lake Geneva

Brick Church Rd.

Fontana Blvd.

Bollinger Rd.

Beloit St.

**WALWORTH**

Dewey Rd.

Townline Rd.

**67**

**14**

**SHARON**

**Wisconsin**

**Illinois**

**HOW** to get there — Take Highway 67 to Fontana and follow Fontana Boulevard to the parking lot in front of the gazebo by the lake.

**DIREC-TIONS at a glance**

0.0 Turn right from the Reed Park parking lot in front of the gazebo; turn left onto Fontana Boulevard.

0.4 Turn left onto Valley View Road (Highway 67).

0.7 Turn right onto Dewey Road.

1.6 Turn left onto Townline Road.

2.5 Turn right, then left around Walworth town square.

2.6 Turn right onto Beloit Street.

8.7 Turn left onto Bollinger Road.

10.0 Turn right onto Highway 67.

10.5 Turn right onto County C.

16.1 Turn right onto County X.

17.2 Continue past Highway 14.

19.0 Turn right onto County K.

20.0 Turn left onto Sweet Road.

20.9 Turn right onto Elm Ridge Road.

21.9 Turn left onto S&D Townline Road.

22.6 Continue past County O.

23.8 Turn right onto Ox Lane Road.

24.5 Turn left onto North Walworth Road.

24.8 Turn right onto Six Corners Road.

26.8 Turn left onto Brick Church Road.

28.6 Turn left onto Valley View Road/Highway 67.

28.9 Turn right onto Fontana Boulevard.

29.2 Return to Reed Park parking lot.

# Organizations, and Clubs

Wisconsin is blessed with a solid statewide organization, the Bicycle Federation of Wisconsin, and a collection of clubs that range in size from a few to hundreds of members in communities across the state. What follows is a list of organizations, resources, and clubs with their addresses and/or, where available, telephone numbers, web pages, and e-mail addresses.

Special thanks for compiling this list go to a wonderful Web page, The Bicycling Community Page, that serves Dane County, Wisconsin, as well as the entire state of Wisconsin and the United States with information on bicycling. The page, a project of the Bicycle Transportation Alliance of Dane County, is edited by Scott Rose, sponsored by Budget Bicycle Center, and hosted at DANEnet. The Bicycling Community Page is at http://danenet.wicip.org/bcp

Thanks go also to Paul Lata, of the Menomonee River Century, who was gracious in adding his ride's list of clubs and organizations.

## Organizations

Alliance for Future Transit
P.O. Box 92056
Milwaukee, WI 53202

Bicycle Federation of Southeastern
Wisconsin
P.O. Box 480
Milwaukee, WI 53201
(414) 375–6180
e-mail: bfsewis@aol.com

Bicycle Federation of Wisconsin
P.O. Box 1224
Madison, WI 53701
(608) 251–4456
e-mail: BFW@mailbag.com

Bicycle Transportation Alliance of
Dane County
Box 641
Madison, WI 53701

Capital Community Citizens
222 South Hamilton Street,
Suite 100
Madison, WI 53703
(608) 256–0565

New Transportation Alliance
c/o Sierra Club
222 South Hamilton Street, Suite 1
Madison, WI 53703
(608) 274–3585 (608) 251–9164
(608) 249–9016

Parents Encouraging Driving Safely
4406 White Aspen Road
Madison, WI 53704
(608) 244–6109

Red Bikes Project
c/o Jillian Corbett
1220 Rutledge Street, #1
Madison, WI 53703

(608) 256–6340
RIDE (Recreation for Individuals
Dedicated to the Environment)
208 South LaSalle, Suite 1808
Chicago, IL 60604

Wisconsin Department of Natural Resources
Bureau of Parks and Recreation
P.O. Box 7921
Madison, WI 53707–7921
(608) 266–0004
e-mail: grubeb@dnr.state.wi.us

Wisconsin Department of Tourism
123 West Washington Avenue
P.O. Box 7976
Madison, WI 53707;
(800) 432–TRIP
(800) 372–2737 from Wisconsin and
neighboring states
http://tourism.state.wi.us

Wisconsin Department of
Transportation Bicycle Safety
Program
OTS Room 809
P.O. Box 7910
4802 Sheboygan Avenue
Madison, WI 53707
(608) 267–3155

Wisconsin Environmental Initiative
5315 Wall Street, Suite 235
Madison, WI 53704–7939
(608) 249–5834

# Clubs

Antigo Bike & Ski Club
1205 Arctic Street
Antigo, WI 54409

Arrow Bicycle Club
2916 Bond Place
Janesville, WI 53545

Bayshore Bicycle Club
P.O. Box 1881
Green Bay, WI 54305–1881

Bay View Bicycle Club
P.O. Box 7455
Milwaukee, WI 53207
(414) 483–7171

Belle City Bicycle Club
5217 Athens Avenue
Racine, WI 53406

Bombay Bicycle Club of
Madison, Inc.
P.O. Box 45685
Madison, WI 53744

Cream City Cycle Club
P.O. Box 894
Milwaukee, WI 53201
hotline: (414) 476–1020

Folks 'n' Spokes
2801 Park Ridge
Marinette, WI 54143
(715) 735–9361

Fox Valley Wheelmen
P.O. Box 4034
Appleton, WI 54915

Great Bicycle Rides across
Wisconsin
Box 310
Spring Green, WI 53588
(608) 935–RIDE
e-mail: wisbike@mhtc.net

Hayward Bicycle Club
P.O. Box 1060
Seeley, WI 54843

LaCrosse Wheelmen
924½ Caledonia Street
LaCrosse, WI 54603
(608) 782–4630

Lake Michigan Wheelmen
1718 Poplar Avenue
South Milwaukee, WI 53172

Lakeshore Pedalers
1037 28th Street
Two Rivers, WI 54241

League of Wisconsin Wheelmen
8057 North 45th Street
Brown Deer, WI 53233

Ozaukee Bicycle Club
P.O. Box 755
Cedarburg, WI 53012

New Pedalers Bike Club
333 West State
Milwaukee, WI 53202

North Roads Bicycle Club
307 West Newton
Rice Lake, WI 54868

Out Spokin' Adventures
409 North Court Street
Sparta, WI 54656
(608) 269–6087 or (800) 4WE–BIKE

Pedal across Wisconsin
P.O. Box 365
Dundee, IL 60118
(708) 695–7964

PowWow Bicycle Tours
3533 West Lapham Street
Milwaukee, WI 53215
Dennis Northey: (414) 671–4560

The Rock Trail Coalition (Janesville)
Dean Painter: (608) 364–3355 or
(608) 756–1832

Sheboygan Co. Bicycling Club
724 Mayflower Avenue
Sheboygan, WI 53083

Spring City Spinners
P.O. Box 2055
Waukesha, WI 53187

Two Tyred Wheelmen
427 West Main Street, #207
Madison, WI 53703

Wa Du Shuda Bike Club
W8365 Highway C
New Lisbon, WI 53950

Wausau Wheelers
P.O. Box 1381
Wausau, WI 54402
(715) 845–5730 or (715) 359–9338

Winnebago Riders
905 Mequon Avenue
Fond du Lac, WI 54935

Wisconsin Off-Road Bicycling
Association
P.O. Box 1681
Madison WI 53701
(608) 251–4911

Women on Wheels
(608) 241–8239

Wood Spokes Bicycle Club
1202 South Central Avenue
Marshfield, WI 54449
(715) 384–8313 or
(715) 387–2763

# Annual Wisconsin Bike Rides

The following is a list, by month, of organized bike rides held annually in Wisconsin. Although every effort has been made to provide a contact address and/or telephone number that will be in place in the future, it's possible that organizers and events might have changed or rides have been canceled. Use this as a guide, not gospel.

**May**

*Appleton*
Intruders Clean Air Tour
Intruders Racing Team
316 North Appleton Street
Appleton, WI 54911
Milhaupt's Bike Works:
(414) 734–1405
15, 30, or 62 miles

*Burlington*
Chocolate City Bike Ride
Bob's Pedal Pusher
456 Milwaukee Avenue
Burlington, WI 53105
(414) 763–7794
18, 31, or 65 miles

*Green Bay*
Tour de Cure Bike the Bay
American Diabetes Association
1600 Shawano Avenue, #210E
Green Bay, WI 54303
(414) 498–1066   (800) TOUR–888
25, 50 or 100 kilometers

*Janesville*
Rock 50/50 Bike Tour
Rock Trail Coalition
P.O. Box 8101

Janesville, WI 53545
(608) 756–2651  (608) 756–1832
50 miles or 50 kilometers

*Madison*
Gear Up Madison
Bombay Bicycle Club
(608) 241–3460
8, 15, and 29 miles

Syttende Mai 64
Bombay Bicycle Club
Norm Dullum:
(608) 222–6047
32 or 64 miles

*Marinette*
Wild Asparagus Ride
Folks 'n' Spokes
Jim Shane
2801 Park Ridge
Marinette, WI 54143
(715) 735–9361
length of ride varies; changes each year

*Mequon*
Tour de Cure
American Diabetes  Association
2949 North Mayfair Road, #306

Wauwatosa, WI 53222
(414) 778–5500  (800)TOUR–888
25, 50, or 100 kilometers

*Northern Kettle Moraine*
American Heart Association Heart
Ride of Washington County
American Heart Association
795 Van Buren Street
Milwaukee, WI 53202–3883
(800) 242–9236
100, 50, or 15 kilometers

*Southern Kettle Moraine*
Phantom Lake YMCA Camp Metric
Century
Attention: Bicycle Tour
Phantom Lake YMCA Camp
P.O. Box 228
Mukwonago, WI 53149
(414) 363–4FUN
20, 35, or 65 miles

*Sparta*
Black Rendezvous
Out Spokin' Adventures
409 North Court Street
Sparta, WI 54656
(608) 269–6087  (800) 4WE–BIKE
60 miles

*Trempealeau*
Spring Bicycle Tour
Trempealeau Chamber of
Commerce, Inc.
P.O. Box 212
Trempealeau, WI 54661
(608) 534-6780
45, 25, or 10 miles

*Wausau*
Spin into Spring Road Ride,
Wausau Wheelers
P.O. Box 1381
Wausau, WI 54402–1381

(715) 359–9338
5 to 30 miles

**June**
*Amherst*
Ragin' Rooster Self-Guided Tour
RRRRT
1813 Waunona Way
Madison, WI 53713
(608) 224–0381
aegraf@inxpress.net.
100 kilometers

*Blanchardville*
Blanchardville Bike-A-Thon
Wildberry Ridge
P.O. Box 68
Blanchardville, WI  53516
(608) 523–2300
8 to 50 miles

*Blue Mounds*
Blue Mounds Classic
Mark Lovejoy
1722 Baker Avenue
Madison, WI 53705
(608) 238–1132
28 miles

*Denmark*
Tour de World
Wayne Paider/Dale Tease
1412 Grighan Street
Green Bay, WI 54301
(414) 435–5837   (414) 497–3583
30 or 60 miles

*Door County*
Ridges Ride for Nature
Ridges Sanctuary
2912 Lake Forest Park Drive
Sturgeon Bay, WI 54235
(414) 743–8138
e-mail: cschuste@mail.wisnet.net
25, 50, or 100 kilometers

*Dunn County*
Dunn County Heart Ride
American Heart Association
2000 Oxford Avenue, Suite 2
Eau Claire, WI 54703
(715) 834–1108  (800) AHA–USA1
6, 16, or 28 miles

*Fond du Lac*
Walleye Weekend E-Z Weekend
Bob Matteson
Fondy Bicycle Club
122 North Bell Street
Fond du Lac, WI 54935
(414) 921–5504 evenings;
(414) 921–8315 days
5, 18, or 35 miles

*Fox River Valley*
Powwow Bicycle Tours
3533 West Lapham Street
Milwaukee, WI 53215
(414) 671–4560
Week-long, 367-mile tour

*Frederic*
Frederic Lions Bike Classic
Frederic Lions Bicycling Classic
Box 563
Frederic, WI 54837
(800) 919–1141, (715) 327–8750,
(715) 653–2331
10, 25, or 56 miles

*Green Bay-Kewaunee*
Shore to Shore 64
Lois Dunn
Family Violence Center, Inc.
P.O. Box 727
Green Bay, WI 54305
(414) 435–0100
64, 35, and 10 miles

*La Crosse*
Killer Hill 64
James Asfoor

c/o LaCrosse Wheelmen
924½ Caledonia Street
LaCrosse, WI 54603
(608) 782–4630
64 miles

*Madison*
Great Dane Fun & Tasty Tour
GDVC
699 West Mifflin Street, #118
Madison, WI 53703
(608) 250–9338
64, 40, or 18 miles

**Tour de Cure**
American Diabetes Association
2949 North Mayfair Road, #306
Wauwatosa, WI 53222
(414) 788–5500
25, 50, or 100 kilometers

*Marinette*
Menominee River Century
Paul Lata
P.O. Box 512
Marinette, WI 54143
(800) 447–5613  (715) 735–7683
15, 40, 80, or 110 miles

*Marshfield*
Dan Jansen Miracle Miles
Sherre Rosandich
Marshfield Clinic
1000 North Oak Avenue
Marshfield, WI 54449
(800) 782–8581
50, 10, or 2 miles

*Milwaukee*
Fat Tire Tour of Milwaukee
(414) 453–9094
25 miles, with on-road option

Miller Lite Ride for the Arts
UPAF
929 North Water Street

**235**

Milwaukee, WI 53202
(414) 276–RIDE
5 to 50 miles; Midwest's largest bike ride

**Neillsville**
Neillsville Bike Tour
Tom Opect
216 Sunset Place
Neillsville, WI 54456
(715) 743–3101, extension 127  .
55 or 20 miles

**Newburg**
River Edge Nature Ride
Riveredge Nature Center
4458 West Hawthorne Drive
P.O. Box 26
Newburg, WI 53060
(414) 675–6888
8, 16, 30, or 50 miles

**Osceola**
Cascade Classic Ride or Race
Osceola Lion's Club
Box 36
Osceola, WI 54020
(715) 294–2603   (715) 755–3277
30 miles

**Southern Wisconsin**
Trek 100 Wisconsin
MACC Fund/Midwest Athletes against Childhood Cancer
250 Bishops Way, Suite 200
Brookfield, WI 53005
(800) 248–TREK   (414) 821–5433
100 mile, 100-kilometer, or 30 mile loop

**Southwest Wisconsin**
Tour of the Mississippi River Valley
Quad Cities Bicycle Club
c/o Susie LaForce
2023 East 45th Street
Davenport, IA 52807

(319) 355–5530
106, 86, 63, or 41 miles through Illinois, Wisconsin, and Iowa

**Sparta**
Slippery Seat Seventy
Olga McAnulty
Sparta Cycling Club
409 North Court Street
Sparta, WI 54656
(608)269–6087   (608) 269–4064
70 or 35 miles

**Spring Green**
GRABAAWR
P.O. Box 310
Spring Green, WI 53588
(608) 935–RIDE
Week-long, 500-mile tour along Wisconsin River; 50–80 miles daily  .

**Stevens Point**
Midwest Recumbent Rally
Hostel Shoppe
929 Main Street
Stevens Point, WI 54481
(800) 233–4340
(715) 341–BIKE in state
Seminars and rides

**Waupaca**
Hartman Creek Metric Century
Waupaca Chamber of Commerce or Harbor Bike & Ski
112 South Main Street
Waupaca, WI 54981
Harbor Bike: (715) 258–5404
up to 60 miles

**Wausau**
Hammerdown Century
Wausau Wheelers
P.O. Box 1381
Wausau, WI 54402–1381
(715) 359–9338   (715) 693–2338
25, 50, 100 kilometers

**July**
*Amherst*
Cloverleaf Century
Hostel Shoppe
929 Main Street
Stevens Point, WI 54481
(715) 341–4340
30, 60, or 100 kilometers

*Burlington*
Heatstroke 100
Bob's Pedal Pusher
456 Milwaukee Avenue
Burlington, WI 53105
(414) 763–7794
Community Education Department:
(414) 763–0219
12, 18, 30, 65, or 100 miles

*Greenwood*
Dairy Days 30
Lonna Klinke
Dairy Days 30
119 North Andrews
Greenwood, WI 54437
(715) 267–6205
28-mile tour, 36-mile race

*Kickapoo Valley*
Out Spokin' Adventures
409 North Court Street
Sparta, WI 54656
(608) 269–6087  (800) 4WE–BIKE
Three days; 40-mile daily average

*Merrill*
Impulse Century and Family Ride
Chris Black
15280 Highway K South
Merrill, WI 54452
(715) 536–1928
e-mail: Blackc@Apexcomm.net
62, 25, or 15 miles

*Milwaukee*
Bay View Cycle Club Classic
Kathy Kissinger
Bay View Bicycle Club
P.O. Box 7455
Milwaukee, WI 53207
(414) 483–7171
62.5, 30, or 15 miles

**Humana Heart Ride**
Sherry A. McNeir
American Heart Association
795 North Van Buren Street
Milwaukee, WI 53202
(800) 242–9236   (414) 271–9999
15, 35, 67, and 100 miles

*Milwaukee to Door County*
Scenic Shore 150
Leukemia Society
1126 South Seventh Street
Suite N-405A
Milwaukee, WI 53214
John Quinette: (800) 261–7399
Two days; 75 miles per day

*Pardeville*
Pedal across Wisconsin
P.O. Box 365
Dundee, IL 60118
(847) 695–7964
Two days; 25, 35, 44, or 78 miles
each day

*Southwest Wisconsin*
Powwow Hidden Valleys Tour
Powwow Bicycle Tours
3533 West Lapham Street
Milwaukee, WI 53215
Dennis Northey: (414) 671–4560
Two days; 160–200 miles

*Trempealeau*
Catfish 50
Sandy Hilton
N13143 Schubert Road

Trempealeau, WI 54661
(608) 534–6890
Deb Lakey: (608) 534–6704
25-mile tour or 50-mile race

*Washington, Milwaukee, and*
 *Ozaukee Counties*
Bike-A-Thon
American Cancer Society
11401 West Watertown Plank Road
Wauwatosa, WI 53037
(414) 453–4500
63, 32, or 10 miles

*West Bend*
Cedar Lake Cycling Classic
Ozaukee Bicycle Club
P.O. Box 755
Cedarburg, WI 53012
(414) 377–4789   (414) 268–0439
30 miles


**August**
*Chilton*
Ledge View Escarpment Tour
Dan Clausen
Calumet Nature Studies
c/o Ledge View Nature Center
P.O. Box 54
Chilton, WI 53014
(414) 849–7094
Four loops; 10 to 30 miles each

*Chippewa Falls*
Tour De Chippewa
Chippewa Falls Kiwanis
P.O. Box 434
Chippewa Falls, WI 54729
(800) 492–2823
25, 50, 75, or 100 miles

*Fort Atkinson*
Tour De Fort Metric Century
Gary Gramley

6 Milwaukee Avenue East
Fort Atkinson, WI 53538
(414) 563–8337
15, 33, or 66 miles

*Fountain City*
Turtle Tour
Merrick State Park Turtle's
S2965 State Road 35
Fountain City, WI 54629
(608) 687–4936
13, 26, or 31 miles

*Grand View*
Firehouse 50
P.O. Box 80
Grand View, WI 54539
(715) 763–3333
50-mile tour, road race, or time trial

*Hales Corners*
Cream City Cycle Club Century Classic
Cream City Cycle Club
P.O. Box 894
Milwaukee, WI 53201–0894
(414) 671–4560
hotline: (414) 476–1020 box 50
55, 70, or 100 miles

*Manitowoc Area*
Powwow Encore
PowWow Bicycle Tours
3533 West Lapham Street
Milwaukee, WI 53215
Dennis Northey: (414) 671–4560
Three days; 150-200 miles

*Manitowoc & Sheboygan*
 *Counties*
Ice Age Century
Lakeshore Pedalers
Attention: Joe
1719 12th Street
Two Rivers, WI 54241

(800) 627–4896   (414) 682–7302
(414) 793–4449
100, 64, or 32 miles

*Mazomanie*
Mazomanie Bike Tour
Mazomanie Community Corporation
P.O. Box 142
Mazomanie, WI 53560
(608) 795–2117
50 or 100 miles

*Mellen*
Penokee Range Bike Race-Tour
Mellen Chamber of Commerce
c/o J. Nix
P.O. Box 793
Mellen, WI 54546
(715) 274–2330
46 miles

*Monroe County*
Monroe County Century Challenge
Olga McAnulty
Sparta Cycling Club
409 North Court Street
Sparta, WI 54656
(608) 269–6087   (800) 354–BIKE
30-, 50-, or 100-mile tour;
100-mile race

*SAGBRAW*
Bike Ride across Wisconsin
Wheel & Sprocket
6955 North Port Washington Road
Glendale, WI 53217
(414) 247–8100
Five days; 40-70 miles per day

*Sharon*
Roun'da Manure
Roger or Debbie Henning
Sharon Historical Society
P.O. Box 711
Sharon, WI 53585
(414) 736–9229

e-mail: debbyh@bossnt. com
15, 30, 45, 60, or 100 miles

*Sheboygan*
Heart Ride
Bob Bourguignon
American Heart Association
790-B Lakeview Road
Green Bay, WI 54304-5779
(800) AHA–USA1
15, 35, 55, or 75 miles

*Southwest Wisconsin*
Tri-State Metric Century
LaCrosse Wheelmen
James Asfoor
924½ Caledonia Street
LaCrosse, WI 54603
(608) 782–4630
100 kilometers

*Spring Green*
Great Spring Green Bicycling
Adventure
Great Bicycle Rides Across
Wisconsin
Box 310
Spring Green, WI 53588
(608) 935–RIDE
e-mail: wisbike@mhtc.net
Two days; options up to 60 miles

*Statewide to King*
King Bike Tour
BVNEW Inc.
1484 Farlin Avenue
Green Bay, WI 54302–1940
(414) 437–9709
Five days; 65 to 70 miles daily

*Statewide to Neillsville*
Highground Tour
The Highground
P.O. Box 457
Neillsville, WI 54456–0457
(715) 743–4224

fax: (715) 743–4324
Three or four days; 120 to 300 miles

### Three Lakes
Nicolet Wheel-A-Way
Three Lakes Information Bureau
P.O. Box 268
Three Lakes, WI 54562
(800) 972–6103
35 or 45 miles

### Waukesha to Whitewater
National MS Society
Wisconsin Chapter
W223 N608 Saratoga Drive,
Suite 110

Waukesha, WI 53186–0401
(414) 547–8999  (800) 242–3358
Two days; 150 miles

### Wausau
Eau Claire Dells Century
Wausau Wheelers
P.O. Box 1381
Wausau, WI 54402
(715) 845–5730 (715) 359–9338
100 miles or 100, 50, or
25 kilometers

### Wisconsin Rapids
The Paper Route
Bob Walker
Flatland Fandies Bicycle Club
2831 Piney Avenue
Wisconsin Rapids, WI 54494
(715) 423–4265
e-mail: walker923@aol.com
10 or 70 miles

### September
*Appleton*
Janus Gourmet Bike Tour
Best Friends of Neenah/Menasha
181 East North Street, Suite 225

Neenah, WI 54956
(414) 729–5600
15, 35, or 70 miles

### Crivitz
Tour de Colour
MCCCSA Tour de Colour
P.O. Box 242
Crivitz, WI 54114
(715) 854–3231
28-mile poker ride

### Door County
Door County Century Weekend
Door County Century
c/o Bob Gaie
1228 Marquette Street
Green Bay, WI 54304
(414) 494–4262
30, 50, 75, or 100 miles

### Fontana
Tour du Lac
American Lung Association
One Point Place, Suite 100
Madison, WI 53719
(608) 833–4555
20, 40, 60, or 100 miles

### Green Bay
Schneider Bike-Run
hotline: (414) 592–3889
20-kilometer bike ride

### La Crosse
Oktoberfest 100
Jim Asfoor
La Grosse Wheelmen
924 /2 Caledonia Street
La Crosse, WI 54603
(608) 782–4630
100 miles or 100 kilometers

### Maple
Maple Fireball
Gregory St. Ogne

4835 South Mill Loop Road
Maple, WI 54854
(715) 363–2507
32-mile tour; 36-mile race

*Marshfield*
Cranberry Century
Wood Spokes Bicycle Club
1202 South Central Avenue
Marshfield, WI 54449
(715) 384–8313 (715) 387–2763
3, 20, 64, or 100 miles

*Merrill*
Colorama Bike Tour
Greg Stezenski, Director,
Parks and Recreation
1004 East First Street
Merrill, WI 54452
(715) 536–7313
30 or 50 miles

*Milwaukee-Chicago*
Great Chicago to Milwaukee
Bike Ride
Thresholds Homeless Program
2700 North Lakeview
Chicago, IL 60614
(312) 472–4581
25, 62, or 100 miles

*Mineral Point*
Wisconsin Heritage Bicycle Tour
Great Bicycle Rides Across
Wisconsin
Box 310
Spring Green, WI 53588
(608) 935–RIDE
e-mail: wisbike@mhtc.net
Two days; options up to 50 miles

*Mount Horeb to Spring Green*
Wright Stuff Century
Bombay Bicycle Club Century Ride
33 University Square, #213

Madison, WI 53715
(608) 251–5674
100, 60, or 30 miles

*New Glarus*
New Glarus Fall Fantasy
Pedal across Wisconsin
P.O. Box 365
Dundee, IL 60118
(708) 695–7964.
Two days; 25, 35, 45, or 75 miles
each day

*Oconto Falls*
Falls Fun Fest Bike Tour
P.O. Box 70
Oconto Falls, WI 54154
(414) 829–5141
25 or 45 miles

*Rome*
Movin' in the Right Direction
St. Luke's Evangelical Church
W1956 Main Street
Rome, WI 53178
(414) 593–2380
12.5 miles

*Waukesha*
SCAT Ride
SCAT
P.O. Box 2055
Waukesha, WI 53187
(414) 297–9135 (414) 544–5921
30 or 64 miles

October
*Eagle River*
Cranberry Fest Bike Ride
Eagle River Chamber of Commerce
P.O. Box 1917
Eagle River, WI 54521
(715) 479–6400 (715) 479–0373
8, 13, or 25 miles

*Galesville*
Apple Affair Bike Tour
c/o Mark Heal
P.O. Box 214
Galesville, WI 54630
(608) 582–4612
30-, 42-, 50-, or 62-mile loops

*Marinette*
Fall Color Ride
Jim Shane
Spokes & Folks
2801 Parkridge
Marinette, WI 54143
(715) 735–9361

*Mayville*
Audubon Classic Bike Ride
Pauline Ellington
Mayville Chamber of Commerce
P.O. Box 185
Mayville, WI 53050
(414) 387–5776 days
(414) 387–4812 evenings
14, 25, or 35 miles

*Reedsburg*
Senior Citizen 400 Trail Ride
Friends of the 400
(800) 844–3507
length of ride varies; changes each
year

*Richland Center*
Ocooch Mountain Fall Bicycle Tour
(OMFBT)
c/o Richland Medical Center
1313 West Seminary
Richland Center, WI 53581
(608) 647–6161
10, 30, or 50 miles

*Siren*
Gandy Dancer Metric Century
Burnett County Historical Society
P.O. Box 31
Siren, WI 54872
(715) 349-2219  (800) 788-3164
15 or 66 miles